Roots of the RUSSIAN Language

Roots of the RUSSIAN Language

George Z. Patrick, Ph.D.

PASSPORT BOOKS
a division of *NTC Publishing Group*
Lincolnwood, Illinois USA

1994 Printing

Published by Passport Books, a division of NTC Publishing Group,
© 1989, 1981 by NTC Publishing Group, 4255 West Touhy Avenue,
Lincolnwood (Chicago), Illinois 60646-1975 U.S.A.
Manufactured in the United States of America.

4 5 6 7 8 9 ML 9 8 7

FOREWORD

Based on the supposition that familiarity and practice with the component elements of Russian words will facilitate student comprehension and learning, *Roots of the Russian Language* includes four hundred and fifty of the most commonly used roots of the Russian language in a convenient, reference format. Mastery of these roots should enable students to form many more derivatives, increasing their Russian vocabularies, as well as enhancing their enjoyment and satisfaction in learning the Russian language.

Once students achieve an understanding and mastery of the basic Russian suffixes and prefixes, they will be able to recognize, identify, and decipher words into their component parts. With this skill established, they should also develop an ability to construct many words and terms from a given Russian root, facilitating both the translation of Russian literature and student conversation and composition.

The phrases that follow the derivatives and compounds in this book are designed to illustrate the proper use of the given word in a realistic sentence. In addition, "Exercises for Practice" is intended to furnish more extended practice in word-building. *Roots of the Russian Language* provides students with the opportunity to acquire a comprehensive knowledge of word-building and vocabulary enrichment in the Russian language.

CONTENTS

ROOTS OF THE RUSSIAN LANGUAGE

COMPONENT ELEMENTS OF RUSSIAN WORDS

The component elements of Russian words are:

1. ROOTS AND STEMS
2. INFLECTIONS
3. PREFIXES
4. SUFFIXES

ROOTS. The root of a word is that essential part of it which it possesses in common with a group of cognate words.

Thus, from the root да we get да-ть; да-ва́-ть; вы́-да-ча; за-да́-ча; про-да́-ть; рас-про-да́-жа; с-да́-ча; у-да́-ча and many other cognates.

STEMS. A stem is the form assumed by the root before an inflectional ending is added to it. Examples:

зна́мен-и
зна́мен-ем } знамен is the stem of the noun зна́мя, banner
знамён-а

твори́-шь
твори́-т } твори is the stem of the present tense of твор-и́-ть, to create
твори́-м

Usually the root and the stem differ from each other. Thus, in the first of the two given examples the stem is знамен, while the root is зна; in the second, the stem is твори and the root is твор. There are words, however, in which the root and the stem are the same. For instance:

Нес-у́, I carry. Both root and stem = нес
вед-у́, I lead. Both root and stem = вед

INFLECTIONS. The inflections are the different endings which indicate gender, number, case, and person Examples:
сад, са́д-а, сад-ы́

1

вод-á, вод-ы́, вóд-ы
бе́л-ый, бе́л-ого, бе́л-ые
говор-и́, говор-и́-шь, говор-и́-те

PREFIXES, SUFFIXES.   A prefix is a particle placed at the beginning of a root; a suffix is one placed at the end of it.

Prefixes alter the meanings of words, while suffixes alter their functions.

Thus there is a difference of meaning between да-ть (to give) and про-да́-ть (to sell); between за-да́-ча (problem) and с-да́-ча (change).

On the other hand, suffixes form nouns, adjectives, verbs, and adverbs, and hence change the function of a word, that is, they make it into one part of speech or another.

Thus the root чист becomes a noun in чист-от-а́, an adjective in чи́ст-ый, a verb in чист-и́-ть, and an adverb in чи́ст-о.

Many words have more than one affix. Examples:

при-над‧леж-а́-ть, to belong
ро́д-ств-ен-н-ик, relative

DERIVATIVES, COMPOUNDS

A word derived from one simple word is called a <u>derivative</u> whereas a word formed through the junction of two or more simple words is called a <u>compound</u>. Thus сад-о́в-н-ик (gardener) is a derivative, while сад-о-во́д-ство (horticulture) is a compound (from <u>сад</u>, garden, and <u>вод-и́-ть</u> to cultivate), as is also два-дцат-и-пят-и-ле́т-н-ий, twenty-five years old.

As a rule, compounds formed from two roots are joined by the so-called connective vowels <u>o</u> or <u>e</u>: пар-о-во́з (engine); птиц-е-во́д-ств-о́ (bird-rearing). In the example двадцатипяти- ле́тний the и after два́дцать and пять is not a connective but the sign of the genitive case. In some compound words, however, there is no connective vowel: Но́вгород (Но́вый го́род); Ленингра́д, etc.

Since the Russian Revolution of 1917 a number of compound words have been formed differently. These new compounds may be grouped as follows:

1. Words formed from two or more initial syllables:

нар-ко́м—<u>наро́дный комисса́р</u>;

ком-со-мо́л—<u>Коммунисти́ческий</u> <u>сою́з молодёжи</u>;

сов-хо́з—<u>сове́тское хозя́йство</u>

2. Compounds formed from an initial syllable of one word joined to another word:

стен-газе́та—сте́нна́я газе́та;

зав-шко́лой—заве́дующий шко́лой

3. Compounds formed from initial letters of two or more words:

рик—райо́нный исполни́тельный комите́т;

Тасс—телегра́фное а́гентство сове́тского сою́за

Often compounds are formed from an initial letter, or initial letters, of one or more words and an initial syllable of another:

ОГИЗ—об'едине́ние госуда́рственных изда́тельств;

Татцик—Тата́рский центра́льный исполни́тельный комите́т.

LIST OF THE MOST IMPORTANT SUFFIXES

A. *Noun Suffixes*

(Usually denoting occupation or agent)

-ак, -як	: рыб-а́к, fisherman; чуд-а́к, queer fellow; мор-я́к, seaman.
-ар, -яр	: па́х-ар-ь, ploughman; пе́к-ар-ь, baker; стол-я́р, carpenter.
-ач	: сил-а́ч, strong man; тк-ач, weaver.
-ец	: бо-е́ц, fighter; куп-е́ц, merchant; пе-в-е́ц, singer.
-ик	: муж-и́к, peasant; му́ч-ен-ик, martyr; уч-ен-ик, pupil.
-ок	: езд-о́к, rider; кус-о́к, piece; стрел-о́к, shooter.
-ост-ь, -ест-ь	: глу́п-ост-ь, stupidity; но́в-ост-ь, news; ску́п-ост-ь, stinginess; све́ж-ест-ь, freshness.
-ств, -еств	: вещ-еств-о́, substance; ис-ку́с-ств-о, art; род-ств-о́, relationship.

Note. The suffixes -ост, -ест, -ств, -еств, usually indicate abstract nouns.

-тел	: пис-а́-тел-ь, writer; стро-й-тел-ь, builder; уч-и́-тел-ь, teacher.
-чик	: ма́л-ь-чик, boy; пере-во́д-чик, translator; раз-но́с-чик, peddler.
-щик	: ден-щи́к, orderly; по-став-щи́к, purveyer; ям-щи́к, coachman.

Suffixes denoting diminutives, endearment

-ек	: ку-со́ч-ек (кусо́к), little piece; лист-о́ч-ек (листо́к), leaflet, little leaf.
-еньк	: ма́м-еньк-а, dear mamma; па́п-еньк-а, dear papa.
-оньк	: берёз-оньк-а, little birch tree.
-ец	: у-ро́д-ец, little monster; бра́т-ец, little brother.
-ик	: но́ж-ик, little knife; но́с-ик, small nose, сто́л-ик, small table.

NOTE. In such words as муж-и́к, уч-ен-и́к, the shade of the diminutive has been lost.

-иц	: лу́ж-иц-а, puddle, small pool.
-ка	: но́ж-ка, small foot; ру́ч-ка, small hand, penholder, handle.
-ок, -очек	: го́лос, voice; голос-о́к, голос-о́чек
-ек, -ёчек	: ого́н-ь, fire; огон-ёк, огон-ёчек
-ёнк	: изб-ёнк-а, wretched little hut; лошад-ёнк-а, jade (often deprecatory)
-ишк	: дом-и́шк-о, little house; вор-и́шк-а, little thief.
-онок	: медвеж-о́нок, bear cub.
-ёнок	: гус-ёнок, gosling; жереб-ёнок, colt.
-очк, -ечк	: цеп-о́чк-а, little chain; под-у́ш-ечк-а, small pillow.
-ышк	: со́лн-ышк-о, little sun; зёрн-ышк-о, small grain.

| -ушк | : дéд-ушк-а, (dear) grandfather; бáб-ушк-а, (dear) grandmother; корóв-ушк-а, dear little cow. |

Suffixes having an augmentative force

| -ин | : дет-ѝн-а, big fellow; дуб-ѝн-а, big cudgel. |
| -ищ | : дом-ѝщ-е, huge house; руч-ѝщ-а, large hand. |

The most important suffix having a collective meaning

| -ь | : баб-ь-ё, womenfolk, females.
мужич-ь-ё, rustics, peasants.
тряп-ь-ё, rags, tatters. |

Suffixes denoting nationality, religion, patronymics

-ак, -як	: пол-я́к, Pole; прусс-áк, Prussian; сибир-я́к, Siberian.
-анин	: англич-áнин, Englishman; магомет-áнин, Mohammedan.
-янин	: христи-анѝн, Christian; слав-янѝн, Slav.

NOTE. In the plural the -ин is dropped:

англич-áн-е, магомет-áн-е, христи-áн-е, слав-я́н-е

-ец	: америкáн-ец, American; нéм-ец, German; япóн-ец, Japanese.
-ович, -евич	: Петр-óвич, son of Peter Николá-евич, son of Nicholas
-овна, -евна	: Петр-óвна, daughter of Peter Николá-евна, daughter of Nicholas.

Suffixes indicating the feminine gender

-ачк, -ячк	: рыб-áчк-а, fishwife; чуд-áчк-а, queer woman; мор-я́чк-а, sailor (f.); сибир-я́чк-а, Siberian.
-их-а	: куп-ч-ѝх-а(купéц); ткач-ѝх-а; повар-ѝх-а, cook.
-иц	: уч-ен-ѝц-а, пис-á-тел-ьн-иц-а; пере-вóд-ч-иц-а

-к	: америка́н-к-а; англича́н-к-а; христиа́н-к-а; сила́ч-к-а, strong woman.
-ух	: стар-у́х-а, old woman; молод-у́х-а, young woman; стряп-у́х-а, cook.

Suffix denoting place

ищ	: жил-и́щ-е, abode, dwelling place; клад б-ищ-е, cemetery; при-ста́-н-ищ-е, refuge, shelter.

B. *Adjective Suffixes*

-ат	: бог-а́т-ый, rich; крыл-а́т-ый, winged; син-ев-а́т-ый, bluish; бел-ов-а́т-ый, whitish.
-ен, -ьн	: бо́л-ен, бол-ьн-о́й, sick, ill
-ист	: золот-и́ст-ый, of golden color серебр-и́ст-ый, silvery.
-к	: гро́м-к-ий, loud; то́н-к-ий, thin; у́з-к-ий, narrow.
-л	: ки́с-л-ый, sour; спе́-л-ый, ripe; тёп-л-ый, warm.
н	: бе́д-н-ый, poor; дур-н-о́й, bad; му́т-н-ый, muddy.
-ов, ев	: берег-ов-о́й, coastal; ключ-ев-о́й, spring; пол-ев-о́й, field; ро́з-ов-ый, rose.
-овск, -евск	: отц-о́вск-ий, father's; поп-о́вск-ий, priest's; корол-е́вск-ий, king's; ки́-евск-ий, of Kiev.
-ск,-еск,-ьск	: ру́с-ск-ий, Russian; де́т-ск-ий, infantile, child's; ю́нош-еск-ий, adolescent, youthful; прия́тел-ьск-ий, friend's, friendly; учи́тель-ск-ий, teacher's.
-ян, -ан	: гли́н-ян-ый, clay; ко́ж-ан-ый, leather

Suffixes denoting diminutives

-еньк	: ма́л-еньк-ий, small; хоро́ш-еньк-ий, pretty, nice
-оньк	: лёг-оньк-ий, light; ти́х-оньк-ий, quiet

Suffixes that convey comparative and superlative degrees

-ее	: бо́л-ее, more; ме́н-ее, less; добр-е́е, kinder
-айш	: велич-а́йш-ий, the biggest, greatest; тонч-а́йш-ий, the thinnest
-ейш	: добр-е́йш-ий, the kindest; скор-е́йш-ий, the quickest
-ьш	: бо́л-ьш-ий, the bigger; наи-бо́л-ьш-ий, the biggest

C. *Verb Suffixes*

-а	: бр-а́-ть, to take; де́л-а-ть, to do; чит-а́-ть, to read
-ва	: да-ва́-ть, to give; от-кры-ва́-ть, to open; с-кры-ва́-ть, to conceal
-е	: вид-е-ть, to see; лет-е́-ть, to fly; смотр-е́-ть, to look
-и	: говор-и́-ть, to speak; люб-и́-ть, to love; прос-и́-ть, to beg
-ну	: гля(д)-ну́-ть, to look; дви́(г)-ну-ть, to move; мо́к-ну-ть, to soak
-ов, -ев	: пир-ов-а́ть, to feast; гор-ев-а́ть, to grieve
-у, -ю	: сове́т-у-ю, I advise; пир-у́-ет, he (or she) feasts; гор-ю́-ю, I grieve
-ыв, -ив	: о-пи́с-ыв-а-ть, to describe; раз-гова́р-ив-а-ть, to converse

D. *Participle Suffixes*

-ащ, -ящ	: (Suffixes of the present participle active)
-ущ, ющ	: держ-а́щ-ий, holding; люб-я́щ-ий, loving; вед-у́щ-ий, leading; чит-а́-ющ-ий, reading
-вш, -ш	: (Suffixes of the past participle active) чит-а́-вш-ий, having read; нёс-ш-ий, having carried
-ен, -н, -т	: (Suffixes of the past participle passive) у-нес-ён, carried away; про-чи́т-а-н, read; про-чи́т-а-нн-ый, read; мы́-т-ый, washed

м   : (Suffix of the present participle passive)
люб-и́-м, люб-и́-м-ый, one who is loved

PREFIXES

These are either separable or inseparable. Prefixes which
are used as independent words are called separable; those
which have no independent existence are called inseparable.

Words formed with prefixes might be called "compounds";
in fact, they are often so designated for convenience. But the
name "Compound" is usually restricted to those words of
which the component parts are nouns, adjectives, or verbs;
whereas the name "Separable prefix" is for the most part
restricted to adverbs and prepositions.

LIST OF PREPOSITIONS USED AS PREFIXES

Only some of the important shades of meaning can be given
here. It must be remembered that most of the prepositions
are used merely to form a perfective from an imperfective verb;
also that in many cases the original meaning of a preposition,
when added to a word, is barely apparent, and in some cases
has even been completely lost.

1. *Separable Prefixes*

без(бес), without, less, dis-, ir-, un-: без-надёжный, hopeless; без-но́гий, without legs; без-упре́чный, irreproachable;
бес-коры́стный, disinterested; бес-поко́ить, to disturb.

When и follows it becomes ы: без-ынтере́сный, uninter-
esting; без-ызве́стность, uncertainty.

NOTE. Before vowels and voiced consonants the prefixes
без, вз, воз, из, низ, раз, роз retain the з; but before unvoiced
consonants and с the з changes into с. Examples:

безбо́жник, atheist; безвы́ходный, hopeless; безгра́мотн-
ость, illiteracy; безда́рный, ungifted; безнра́вственность,
immorality; бесконе́чно, endlessly; беспла́тный, gratis;
бессвя́зный, incoherent; бестолко́вость, fatuity; бесфо́р-
менный, shapeless; бесхара́ктерный, soft, yielding.

в (во), in, into, to:
в-веде́ние, introduction
в-далеке́, in the distance
в-дре́безги, in pieces, to pieces
во-влека́ть, во-вле́чь, to draw in, to involve

до, till, to the end, pre-:
   до-си́живать, to sit up till
   до-ста́ивать, to remain standing to the end
   до-революцио́нный, pre-revolutionary

за, beyond, behind, for:
   за-гро́бный, beyond the grave
   за-позд́алый, belated, behind
   за-чем? Why? What for?

In composition with verbs за often expresses the beginning
of an action:
   заговори́ть, to start talking
   заиграть, to begin to play
   запе́ть, to start singing

из(ис), out of, from:
   из-бира́ть, to elect, to choose
   из-ве́дать, to try out, to find out
   ис-хо́д, issue, outlet
   ис-чеза́ть, to go out of sight, to disappear

между, inter (never used with verbs):
   между-наро́дный, international
   между-ца́рствие, interregnum

на, on, upon:
   на-веща́ть, на-вести́ть, to visit, to call on (upon)
   на-ходи́ть, на-й-ти́, to find, to come upon

(For other shades of meaning see Forbes, Russian Grammar,
p. 238).

над, over, super:
   над-зе́мный, overground
   над-стро́йка, superstructure

о, (об, обо), about, round:
   о-гля́дываться, to look round (about)
   об-води́ть,
   об-вести́, } to lead round

When и follows it becomes ы:
   об-ыгра́ть, to beat (at), to win

от, (ото), away, away from:

от-гоня́ть,
ото-гна́ть, } to drive away
от-ходи́ть,
ото-й-ти́, } to go away from

When и follows it becomes ы:

от-ыгра́ться, to win back (from)

по- Mostly used to make imperfective verbs perfective:
like, a little
проси́ть, по-проси́ть;
у́жинать, по-у́жинать, etc.
по-ба́рски, like a lord; поговори́ть, to have a chat

под(подо), under, underneath:
под-бро́сить, to throw under
под-во́дный, submarine
под-чёркивать, } to underline
под-черкну́ть,

When и follows it becomes ы:

под-ы́грывать, to accompany, to play (while someone is singing)

пред (перед), before, fore, pre-:
пред-обе́денный, before dinner
пред-наме́ренный, premeditated
пред-реша́ть, to foreclose

при- In composition with verbs expresses the idea of motion towards.
при-езжа́ть,
при-е́хать, } to arrive
при-носи́ть,
при-нести́, } to bring

про, through, past:
про-езжа́ть,
про-е́хать, } to pass, to drive through
про-лета́ть,
про-лете́ть, } to fly past

с (со), with, down, off:

с-ближа́ть, с-бли́зить, to draw together, to make friends with
с-бра́сывать, с-бро́сить, to throw down
с-дира́ть, to strip off
с-нима́ть,
с-нять, } to take off

When и follows it becomes ы:

с-ыгра́ть, to play

у, away:

у-езжа́ть, у-éхать, to depart, to go away
у-мира́ть, у-мерéть, to die, to pass away
у-та́скивать, у-тащи́ть, to drag away

2. *Inseparable Prefixes*

воз (вз), вос (вс), up:

воз-двига́ть, to erect, to raise
вз-дорожа́ть, to rise in price
вос-то́к, the East
вс-ходи́ть, to rise
Со́лнце всхо́дит и захо́дит. The sun rises and sets.

вы, out:

вы-води́ть,
вы́-вести, } to lead out
вы-ду́мывать,
вы́-думать, } to invent, devise
вы-пада́ть,
вы́-пасть, } to fall out

It will be observed that вы is accented in perfective compounds, but unaccented in imperfect compounds.

низ, нис, down:

низ-води́ть,
низ-вести́, } to bring down
нис-проверга́ть, нис-провéргнуть, to overthrow
нис-ходи́ть, to descend

пере, пре, over, across, afresh:

пере-води́ть, to translate
пере-да(ва́)ть, to transmit, hand over
пере-езжа́ть, to cross, to come over
пре-восходи́ть, to surpass
пре-ступи́ть, to overstep, to transgress

раз, рас, dis-, di-, un-:
 раз-гибáть, to unbend
 раз-давáть, to distribute
 раз-делúть, to divide
 рас-пускáть,⎫to dissolve, to dismiss
 рас-пустúть,⎭

VARIATION OF VOWELS AND CONSONANTS

The most common changes that may occur in the stem of words of the same derivation are:

VOWELS

o may interchange with a : хóдит, похáживает
            нóсит, вынáшивает

е „   „   „ о, и : наберý, набóр, набирáть
            зáпер, запóр, запирáть

и „   „   „ ой : бить, бой; гнить, гной
ы „   „   „ ов : рыть, ров; крыть, крóвля
   „   „   „ ав : слыть, слáва
у „   „   „ ы : слýшать, слышать
   „   „   „ ов : кую, ковáть
   „   „   „ ев : жую, жевáть

INSERTION OF VOWELS

-ра- often changes into -оро-: град, гóрод
            храм, хорóмы
            прах, пóрох

-ла- „   „   „ -оло-: главá, головá
            власть, вóлость
            хлад, хóлодно

-ре- „   „   „ -ере-: брег, бéрег
            прéдок, перéдний
            дрéво, дéрево

-ле- „   „   „ -еле-(-оло-): плёнка, пеленá
            млéко, молокó
            влекý, волокнó

CONSONANTS

г interchanges with	ж, з		:	друг, дру́жеский, друзья́
д	,,	ж or жд	:	буди́ть, бужу́, пробужде́ние
з	,,	ж	:	моро́зить, моро́женое; ре́зать, ре́жу
к	,,	ч or ц	:	река́, ре́чка, кула́к, кула́цкий
ц	,,	ч	:	столи́ца, столи́чный
х	,,	ш	:	смех, смеши́ть
с	,,	ш	:	носи́ть, ношу́
т	,,	ч or щ	:	свет, свеча́, освеще́ние
ст	,,	щ	:	ме́сто, помеще́ние
ск	,,	щ	:	иска́ть, ищу́
д, т before т change into с			:	веду́, вести́, мету́, мести́, па́дать, пасть

INSERTION OF CONSONANTS

If a root ends in б, п, в, or м, the letter л is usually inserted before ю, е and sometimes before я:

    люби́ть, люблю́, влюблённый
    терпе́ть, терплю́
    лови́ть, ловлю́, ло́вля
    корми́ть, кормлю́, кормле́ние
    дрема́ть, дремлю́, дре́млешь, дремля́

DELETION OF CONSONANTS

д and т are deleted before л, м, and н: па́дать-пал (instead of па-д-л); веду́-вёл (instead of ве-д-л); плету́-плёл (instead of пле-т-л); дам (instead of да-д-м); гляде́ть-гляну́л (instead of гля-д-нул).

б and п are sometimes deleted before н; ги́бнуть, сги́нуть; спать-сон (instead of со-п-н), усну́ть (instead of ус-п-нуть).

в is often deleted after б: облека́ть (instead of об-в-лекать); о́блако (instead of об-в-лако); обя́зан (instead of об-в-язан); о́бласть (instead of об-в-ласть); обы́чай (instead of об-в-ычай), etc.

A
АЛК-, HUNGRY, GREEDY

алк-а́ть, to be hungry, greedy, thirsty, to long for

Они́ а́лчут пи́щи. They are hungry for food.

а́лч-ность, greediness, strong desire, eagerness

Он изве́стен свое́й а́лчностью к деньга́м. He is known for his greediness for money.

а́лч-ный, greedy, hungry

А́лчный челове́к. A greedy man.

а́лч-ущий, hungry, famished

Накорми́те а́лчущих. Feed the hungry.

АУ-, HALLOO, ECHO

ау́-кать, to halloo, shout to each other

Де́ти ау́кают в лесу́. The children are hallooing in the forest.

ау́-кнуть, to halloo, shout, cry out

Кто́-то ау́кнул. Someone hallooed. (Someone cried out.)

ау́-кнуться, to echo, halloo

Как ау́кнется, так и откли́кнется. When one shouts, one's echo comes back. (One good turn deserves another.)

ау́-канье, echo, halloo

И́здали доно́сится ау́канье. The echo reaches from afar.

Б
БА-, TALK, SAYING, CHATTER, TELL STORIES

ба́-сня, fable

Мы прочли́ все ба́сни. We read all the fables.

ба́-сенник, fabulist, fable-maker

Крыло́в изве́стный ба́сенник. Krylov is a well-known fabulist.

ба-снослóвный, fabulous, mythological

Он заплатѝл за дом басно-слóвную цéну. He paid for the house a fabulous price.

бá-ять, to speak, talk

Об э́том бáяли в стáрое врéмя. (They) used to talk about it in ancient times.

ба-ю́кать, to lull

Мать баю́кает ребёнка. The mother lulls (her) child.

у-ба-ю́кать, to lull to sleep

Егó трýдно убаю́кать. It is difficult to lull him to sleep.

БАВ-, AMUSE, ADD, RID

до-бав-ля́ть,⎫
до-бáв-ить, ⎬ to add

Онá добáвила водȳ к сýпу. She added (some) water to the soup.

до-бáв-очный, additional, supplementary

Добáвочная стóимость. Additional cost. Surplus value.

за-бáв-а, amusement, fun

Им всё забáва. Everything is fun to them.

за-бáв-ник, entertaining person

Он большóй забáвник. He is a jolly good fellow.

за-бáв-ный, amusing, entertaining, funny

Какóй забáвный анекдóт. What an amusing anecdote.

за-бав-ля́ться, to amuse oneself, play

Дéти забавля́ются в пáрке. The children are playing in the park.

из-бав-ля́ть,⎫to rid, rescue
из-бáв-ить, ⎬deliver, relieve,
⎭ spare

Избáвьте меня́ от э́той рабóты. Relieve me from this work.

из-бав-ля́ться,⎫
из-бáв-иться, ⎬to get rid

Мы не мóжем от негó избáвиться. We cannot get rid of him.

из-бав-и́тель, liberator, deliverer, rescuer

Он её избави́тель. He is her liberator.

при-бáв-ка, augmentation, increase, raise

Я получѝл прибáвку. I received a raise.

БД-, БОД-, БУД-, AWAKE, VIGIL, WATCH, BRAVE, SOUND

бд-е́ние, vigilance, watchful-ness, evening-service

Мы пошли́ ко всено́щному бде́нию. We went to the evening-service. We went to the vespers.

бд-и́тельноств, watchfulness

Благодаря́ ва́шей бди́тель-ности всё це́ло. Every-thing is safe, thanks to your watchfulness.

бд-и́тельный, watchful, vigil-ant, wide-awake

Бди́тельный наблюда́тель. A wide-awake observer.

бо́д-рость, courage, vigour

Она́ сохрани́ла бо́дрость ду́ха. She has preserved (her) spiritual vigour.

бо́д-рый, brave, sound, heal-thy, hale and hearty

Он ещё бо́дрый стари́к. The old man is still hale and hearty.

бо́д-рствовать, to stay up, to be awake, watch

Несмотря́ на по́здний час они́ ещё бо́дрствуют. In spite of the late hour, they are still up.

буд-и́льник, alarm clock

У меня́ нет буди́льника. I have no alarm clock.

буд-и́ть, to wake, awake, wake up

Пора́ их буди́ть. It's time to wake them up.

бу́д-ни (бу́д-ень), weekday, weekdays

В бу́дни мы рабо́таем. On weekdays we work.

бу́д-ничный, week-day, every-day, working

На нём бу́дничная оде́жда. He wears (his) every-day clothes.

БЕГ-, (БѢГ)-, RUN, FLIGHT

бег, running, course, race, trot

Бы́стрый бег ло́шади. A swift trot of the horse.

бе́г-ать, }to run беж-а́ть, }	На́до скоре́е бежа́ть за до́ктором. We must (It is necessary to) run for the doctor right away.
бе́г-лый, fugitive, deserter, rapid	Э́то бе́глый солда́т. He is a deserter.
бе́г-ство, flight, escape	Неприя́тель обрати́лся в бе́гство. The enemy has turned to flight.
бе́ж-енец, refugee	За-грани́цей мно́го ру́сских бе́женцев. There are many Russian refugees abroad.
из-бег-а́ть, to avoid, shun, escape	Я избега́ю шу́мных у́лиц. I avoid noisy streets.
на-бе́г, invasion, inroad, attack	Росси́я пострада́ла от тата́р-ских набе́гов. Russia suffered from the Tartar invasions.
по-бе́г, escape, flight, deser-tion	Кропо́ткин соверши́л сме́лый побе́г. Kropotkin made a daring escape.
раз бе́г, run, start	Э́тот ров мо́жно перепры́г-нуть с разбе́га. One may jump over (across) this ditch at a run.
пере-беж-а́ть, to run across	За́яц перебежа́л доро́гу. A rabbit ran across the road.
под-беж-а́ть, to run up, come running to	Ма́льчик подбежа́л к отцу́. The boy came running to his father.
при-бе́ж-ище, shelter, re-treat, recourse	Она́ оста́лась без прибе́жища. She was left without a shelter.
с-бе́г-ать, to run, run down	Мне ну́жно сбе́гать в апте́ку. I must run down to the drug store.

у-беж-áть,⎫ to run away, escape   Собáка убежáла со дворá. The dog ran away from the yard.
у-бег-áть, ⎭

у-бéж-ище, asylum, shelter   Убéжище для душéвно-больны́х. An asylum for the mentally deranged people.

БЕД-, (БѢД)-, БИД-, POOR, BAD

бед-á, misfortune, misery, disaster   Бедá однá не прихóдит. Misfortune does not come alone.

бéд-ность, poverty   Бéдность не порóк. Poverty is no crime.

бéд-ный, poor   Бéдный мужи́к. A poor peasant.

бед-óвый, mischievous, unmanageable, dangerous   Какóй он бедóвый. How mischievous he is!

бéд-ствие, calamity, disaster   Наводнéние — большóе бéдствие. Flood is a great disaster.

бéд-ствовать, to be in need, in want, to be poor   Эта семья́ óчень бéдствует. This family is very poor.

по-бéд-а, victory, triumph   Нáши войскá одержáли побéду. Our troops won a victory.

по-бед-и́ть, to conquer, vanquish   Победи́ть врагá не всегдá легкó. It is not always easy to conquer an enemy.

у-бед-и́ть, to convince, induce, persuade   Я не могу́ егó убеди́ть в э́том. In this matter I cannot convince him.

у-бежд-éние, conviction   В э́том моё глубóкое убеждéние. This is my profound conviction about it.

пред-у-бежд-éние, bias, prejudice   Он человéк без предубеждéний. He is a man without prejudice.

о-би́д-а, insult, offense

Вы мне нанесли́ го́рькую оби́ду. You have given me grievous offense.

о-би́д-еть, to offend

Я не хоте́л вас оби́деть. I did not want to offend you.

о-би́д-чик, offender, wrong-doer

Оби́дчика привлекли́ к отве́т-ственности. The offender was put on trial.

о-би́ж-енный, offended, injured

У него́ оби́женный вид. He looks offended.

БЕЛ-, (БѢЛ)-, WHITE

бел-е́ть, to appear white, turn white

Снег беле́ет на горе́. The snow looks white on the mountain.

бел-изна́, whiteness

У нее́ ко́жа необыкнове́нной белизны́. Her skin is of unusual whiteness.

бе́л-ка, squirrel

Бе́лка пры́гает на ве́тке. A squirrel is jumping on a branch.

бел-о́к, white, albumen

Взбе́йте бело́к в пе́ну. Beat the white of an egg into a foam.

бел-ь-ё, linen, underwear

Пра́чка стира́ет бельё. The laundress washes the linen.

бел-ь-мо́, cataract, white spot in the eye

'Он торчи́т, как бельмо́ на глазу́. He stays here like an eyesore.

бел-о-ку́рый, fair-haired, blonde

Белоку́рый ма́льчик. A fair-haired boy.

бел-о-ру́чка, lazy man or woman

Белору́чки не лю́бят мно́го рабо́тать. Lazy people do not like to work hard.

до́-бел-а, at a white heat, white-flame heat

Желе́зо накали́лось добела. The iron is heated to a white heat.

на-бел-о, clean, fair

Перепишйте ва́ше сочине́ние на́бело. Write a clean draft of your composition.

про-бе́л, blank, gap, void, space, short-coming, draw-back

Вы пи́шите с оши́бками — э́то большо́й пробе́л. You write with mistakes; this is a serious (great) draw-back.

БЕРЕГ-, БРЕГ-, GUARD, WATCH, SPARE, BOARD, SHORE

бе́рег, shore, bank

Наш дом на берегу́ реки́. Our house is on the river bank.

береж-ёный, protected, guarded

Бережёного Бог бережёт. Help yourself, and God will help you. (God protects him who protects himself.)

береж-ли́вый, careful, saving, economical, frugal

Она́ бережли́вая же́нщина. She is a frugal woman.

бере́ч-ь (бере́г-ть), to take care of, guard, look after

Здоро́вье ну́жно бере́чь. One must take care of one's health.

на-береж-ная, quay, wharf

Они́ гуля́ли по на́бережной. They walked along the quay.

при-бере́ч-ь, to keep, save, preserve

Прибереги́ оста́тки. Save the remnants.

БЕС-, (БѢС)-, DEMON, DEVIL

бес, demon, devil, tempter

Бес не дре́млет. The devil (tempter) does not sleep.

бес-и́ть, to madden, enrage, drive one mad

Не́чего меня́ беси́ть. Don't you drive me mad.

бес-нова́ться, to storm, rage, to be mad

Стари́к беснова́лся це́лый день. The old man raged all day long.

бе́ш-енство, rage, madness, frenzy, fury

В бе́шенстве он ри́нулся к окну́. He rushed to the window in a frenzy.

бе́ш-еный, mad, rabid, raging, exorbitant

Бе́шеная соба́ка укуси́ла де́вочку. A mad dog bit the little girl.

Они́ заплати́ли за дом бе́шеные де́ньги. They paid an exorbitant price for the house.

БИ-, БОЙ-, BATTLE, BEAT

би-ть, to beat, strike, whip, spank

Не́кому вас бить за ва́ши прока́зы. There is no one to whip you for your pranks.

би-е́ние, beating, beat, palpitation

У неё сла́бое бие́ние пу́льса. Her pulse (beat) is weak.

би́-тва. battle, fight, combat

К ве́черу начала́сь реши́тельная би́тва. A decisive battle began towards the evening.

раз-би-ва́ть,⎫ to break,
раз-би́-ть, ⎭ smash

Он разби́л стака́н. He broke a drinking glass.

раз би́-тый, broken

В разби́тое окно́ ду́ет. There is a draught from the broken window.

у-би-ва́ть,⎫to kill
у-би́-ть, ⎭

Охо́тник уби́л во́лка. The hunter killed the wolf.

у-би́-й-ство, murder

Его́ суди́ли за уби́йство. He was tried for murder.

у-би́-й-ца, murderer, assassin

Уби́йцу отпра́вили в Сиби́рь. They sent the murderer to Siberia.

бой, fight

Ви́дели-ли вы бой быко́в? Did you see a bullfight?

бо́й-кий, bold, daring, energetic

Бо́йкий ма́лый не пропадёт.
An energetic person won't
perish.

бо́й-ня, slaughterhouse, butchery

В го́роде две бо́йни. There
are two slaughterhouses in
the city.

раз-бо́й, robbery

Ведь э́то су́щий разбо́й. But
this is a downright robbery.

раз-бо́й-ник, robber, brigand

Я чита́л расска́з о разбо́й-
никах. I read the story
about the brigands.

БЛАГ- WELL, WELFARE, GOOD, FINE

бла́г-о, good, welfare

Он всё сде́лает для бла́га
наро́да. He will do any-
thing for the welfare of the
people.

благ-о́й, good, favourable

У нас мно́го благи́х поры́вов.
We have many good inten-
tions.

благ-о-дар-и́ть, to thank

Благодарю́ вас. (I) thank
you.

благ-о-да́р-ность, gratitude,
   thanks

Не сто́ит благода́рности.
(Don't mention it.) It is
not worth thanks.

благ-о-да́-ть, blessing, abund-
   ance, peace

Здесь така́я благода́ть! It
is so peaceful here!

благ-о-де́-тель, benefactor

Вы мой благоде́тель. You
are my benefactor.

благ-о-надёжный, trusty, reliable

Это благонадёжный челове́к.
He is a reliable man.

благ-о-ро́дный, noble

Благоро́дный посту́пок. A
noble action (conduct).

благ-о-слови́ть, to bless, to
   give one's blessing

Роди́тели благослови́ли неве́-
сту. The parents gave their
blessing to the bride.

благ-о-состоя́ние, well-being, prosperity, condition

Благосостоя́ние страны́ улу́чшилось. The condition of the country has improved.

БЛЕСК-, БЛЕСТ-, БЛИСТ-, GLISTEN, SHINE

блеск, glitter, lustre, shine

Я́ркий блеск звёзд. The bright glitter of the stars.

о́т-блеск, reflection

О́тблеск зари́ на реке́. The reflection of the sunset on the river.

про́-блеск, flash, spark, ray of light

У него́ мелькну́л про́блеск наде́жды. A spark of hope flashed through his mind.

блест-е́ть, to shine, sparkle

Вода́ блести́т на со́лнце. Water sparkles in the sun.

блес-ну́ть(блеск-ну́ть), to sparkle, shine, flash

Блесну́ла мо́лния. Lightning flashed.

блест-я́щий, bright, shining, brilliant

Ива́н Петро́вич блестя́щий ора́тор. Ivan Petrovich is a brilliant orator.

за-блест-е́ть, to begin to shine, sparkle

Огоньки́ заблесте́ли в тума́не. Lights began to shine in the fog.

блист-а́ть, to shine

Она́ блиста́ла в о́бществе. She shone in (fashionable) society.

блист-а́тельный, splendid, brilliant

Они́ соверши́ли блиста́тельный по́двиг. They performed a splendid feat.

БЛИЗ-, NEAR

близ, near

Близ села́ зелене́ют па́шни. The green fields are near the village.

близ-кий, near, close	Она моя близкая родствен-ница. She is my near relation.
близ-нец, twin	Эти сёстры — близнецы. These sisters are twins.
близ-ость, nearness, prox-imity	Ивы указывали на близость реки. The willows indi-cated the nearness of the river.
близ-о-рукий, near-sighted	Близорукому нужны очки. A near-sighted man needs glasses.
в-близ-й, near-by, not far	Они живут вблизи от нас. They live not far from us.
с-ближ-ение, bringing to-gether, rapprochement	Недавно произошло сближе-ние Японии с Германией. Recently a rapprochement between Japan and Ger-many took place.
с-близ-иться, to become friendly, intimate	Они познакомились и сбли-зились. They got ac-quainted and became inti-mate.

БОГ-, GOD, RICH, WEALTH

бог, God	Слава Богу, вы здоровы. Thank God, you are well!
бож-ество, deity, divinity	Ты божество моё, сказала она. You are my deity, said she.
бож-ий, God's	Я хочу поглядеть на мир Божий. I want to see the world.
бог-а-дельня, almshouse, poorhouse	Выстроили новую богадель-ню. They have built a new almshouse.

бог-о-ро́дица, Our Lady, the Virgin Mary

На стене́ виси́т ико́на Бого-ро́дицы. The Ikon of Our Lady is hanging on the wall.

на́-бож-ный, pious, devout

Она́ на́божна. She is pious.

о-бож-а́ть, to adore

Её обожа́ют де́ти. Children adore her.

у-бо́г-ий, wretched, humble, poor

На краю́ дере́вни стои́т убо́гая ха́та. At the farthest end of the village there is a humble hut.

бог-а́тый, rich, wealthy

Бога́тый бе́дному не ве́рит. The rich do not trust the poor.

бог-аты́рь, giant, hero

В были́нах мы узнаём о ру́сских богатыря́х. In the bylinas we learn about the Russian giants.

раз-бог-ате́ть, to grow rich, become wealthy

В коро́ткое вре́мя он раз-богате́л. In a short time he became wealthy.

БОЛ-, ILL, HURT, PAIN, ACHE

бол-ь, pain, ache

Зубна́я боль мучи́тельна. A toothache is tormenting.

бол-е́знь, illness, disease

Он не мог притти́ по боле́зни. He could not come because of illness.

бол-е́ть, to be ill, sick

Вы ре́дко боле́ете. You are seldom ill.

бол-ь-ни́ца, hospital

Меня́ отвезли́ в городску́ю больни́цу. They took me to the city hospital.

бол-ь-но́й, sick, ill, patient

Больно́й поправля́ется. The patient is recovering.

за-бол-ева́ть, } to fall ill,
за-бол-е́ть, } to be ill

Моя́ мать серьёзно заболе́ла. My mother is seriously ill.

БОЛТ-, CHATTER, TALK, DANGLE

болт-а́ть, to chat, prattle

Весь ве́чер болта́ли об э́том происше́ствии. The entire evening they prattled about this incident.

болт-ли́вый, talkative

Ваш друг сли́шком болтли́в. Your friend is too talkative.

болт-овня́, prattle, gossip

Она́ занима́ется то́лько болтовнёй. She does nothing but gossip.

болт-у́н, chatterbox, chatterer

От э́того болтуна́ все бегу́т. Everyone avoids this chatterbox.

про-болт-а́ться, to babble, to make a slip of the tongue, to blab

Я случа́йно проболта́лся. Inadvertently I blabbed out.

БОЛ-, БОЛЬ-, MORE, LARGE, GREAT

бо́ль-ший, larger, greater

В саду́ я провожу́ бо́льшую часть дня. I spend the greater part of the day in the garden.

боль-шо́й, large, great, big

Мы потеря́ли большо́е состоя́ние. We have lost quite a fortune.

боль-шинство́, majority

Большинство́ призна́ло э́тот зако́н. The majority adopted this law.

боль-шеви́к, Bolshevik

Большевики́ пра́вят Росси́ей. The Bolsheviks rule Russia.

бо-я́рин (бол-я́рин), nobleman

Шу́йский был боя́рином. Shuisky was a nobleman.

бо-я́рский, nobleman's, of nobility

Боя́рская Ду́ма собира́лась ре́дко. The Council of Nobility met rarely.

бо-я́рство, nobility, old nobility

Боя́рство выступа́ло про́тив царя́. The nobility used to come out against the tsar.

БОС-, BARE

бос-о́й, barefoot

Ле́том крестья́не ча́сто хо́дят босы́ми. In summer the peasants often go barefoot.

бос-ико́м, barefoot

Де́ти перешли́ ре́чку босико́м. The children crossed the stream barefoot.

бос-я́к, hobo, tramp

По костю́му э́то был типи́чный бося́к. Judged from his clothes, he was a typical tramp.

БР-, БЕР-, БИР-, БОР-, TAKE, SEIZE, CLIMB, ELECT, COLLECT

бр-ать, to take

Он был вы́нужден брать взя́тки. He was forced to take bribes.

бер-у́, (I) take, I am taking

Я беру́ уро́ки ру́сского языка́. I am taking lessons in Russian.

вз-бир-а́ться, to climb, ascend

Мы с трудо́м взбира́емся на́ гору. We ascend the mountain with difficulty.

взо-бр-а́ться, to climb

Ма́льчики взобра́лись на чердак. The boys climbed into the garret.

вы-бир-а́ть, to choose, select, elect

Рабо́чие выбира́ют делега́тов. The workmen are electing the delegates.

вы́-бр-ать to choose, elect

Мы ещё не вы́брали председа́теля. We have not yet elected the chairman.

за-бо́р, fence, hedge

Не пры́гай че́рез забо́р. Don't jump over the fence.

с-бо́р-ник, collection, anthology

На столе́ лежи́т сбо́рник стихотворе́ний. The anthology of verse is lying on the table.

со-бр-а́ние, meeting

За́втра состои́тся собра́ние в клу́бе. To-morrow there will be a meeting at the club.

БРАТ-, BROTHER

брат, brother

У меня́ нет бра́та. I have no brother.

бра́т-ский, brotherly, brother's

Бра́тская любо́вь крепка́. Brotherly love is strong.

бра́т-ство, brotherhood, fraternity

Свобо́да, ра́венство и бра́тство. Liberty, equality, and fraternity.

брат-а́ться, to fraternize

Он не хо́чет с ни́ми брата́ться. He does not want to fraternize with them.

БРЕД-, БРОД-, WANDER

бред, delirium, raving, frenzy

Тяжёлый бред души́л больно́го. An oppressïve delirium was suffocating the sick man.

бре́д-ить, to rave, to be delirious

Он то́лько э́тим и бре́дит. He simply raves about it.

бре́д-ни, nonsense, dreams, ravings

Всё э́то бре́дни. All this is nonsense.

брод-и́ть, roam, ramble, to wander

Он броди́л по це́лым дням. He was roaming for days.

брес-ти́(бред-ти́), to wander, roam, go slowly

Стару́ха едва́ бредёт. The old woman hardly drags her feet.

брод-я́га, tramp, vagabond

Бродя́га шата́ется из го́рода в го́род. A tramp wanders from city to city.

брод-я́жничать, to prowl, tramp

Безрабо́тные ста́ли бродя́жничать. The unemployed began to prowl about.

брод-я́жничество, prowling, vagrancy

Его́ арестова́ли за бродя́жничество. He was arrested for vagrancy.

с-бро́д, rabble, mob, riff-raff

На окра́ине го́рода живёт вся́кий сброд. All kinds of riff-raff live on the outskirts of the city.

БРОС-, БРАС-, THROW, TOSS

брос-а́ть, to throw, cast, fling

Не броса́йте камне́й в чужо́й огоро́д. Don't throw stones into a stranger's truck-garden. (Don't cast aspersions upon other people.)

бро́с-ить, to throw, give up

Он бро́сил слу́жбу. He gave up the position.

вы-бра́с-ывать, to throw out, cast, reject

Не выбра́сывай всего́ без разбо́ру. Don't throw out everything indiscriminately

вы́-брос-ить, to throw out, away

Да я уже́ всё вы́бросил. But I have already thrown away everything.

на-бра́с-ывать, to sketch, jot, outline

Он всегда́ на́скоро набра́сывает эски́з. He always jots down (his) sketch in a hurry.

на-брос-а́ть, to sketch, throw on, scatter

Ско́лько со́ру наброса́ли на у́лицу. How much rubbish they have thrown on the street.

на-брóс-ить, to throw on, over	Дáма набрóсила шаль на плéчи. The lady threw a shawl over her shoulders.
раз-брáс-ывать, to throw about, scatter	Не разбрáсывайте кни́ги. Do not scatter the books.
раз-брос-áть, to throw about, scatter	Ивáн разбросáл все вéщи и ушёл. Ivan had scattered all his things and gone away.

БУЙ-, БУ-, RAGE, STORM

бýй-ный, stormy, raging, violent	Бýйным вéтром снеслó кры́шу. The raging wind tore off the roof.
бýй-ство, boisterousness, turbulence	Солдáта наказáли за бýйство. The soldier was punished for his boisterousness.
бýй-ство-вать, to rage, storm, behave violently, to be on the rampage	Пья́ный всё врéмя бýйствовал. The drunken man was violent all the time.
бу-нт, revolt, uprising	Он зовёт их на бунт. He calls them to a revolt.
бу-нтовáть, to revolt, rebel	Они́ не хотя́т бунтовáть. They do not want to rebel.
бу-нтовщи́к, rebel, mutineer	Бунтовщики́ разби́ли óкна. The rebels broke the windows.
бу-шевáть, to storm, rage	Мóре бушевáло. The sea raged.

БУР , STORM

бýр-я, storm	Разрази́лась си́льная бýря. A driving storm broke out.
бур-ли́ть, to storm, boil, bubble	Ручéй бурли́т в ущéлье. A stream bubbles in the gorge.

бу́р-ный, stormy, violent, heated — Бу́рное заседа́ние до́лго продолжа́лось. The stormy (heated) conference lasted a long time.

БЫ-, BEING, EXISTENCE

бы-ть, to be, exist — "Быть и́ли не быть, вот в чём вопро́с". To be, or not to be: that is the question.

бы-тие́, existence, being, life, genesis — Мона́х чита́л кни́гу Бытия́. The monk was reading Genesis.

бы-ль, fact, true tale — Э́то быль, а не ска́зка. This is a true tale, not a fairy tale.

бы-ли́на, bylina, Russian folklore, ballad — Мы чита́ли ру́сские были́ны. We were reading the Russian ballads.

бы-т, existence, mode of life, life — Они́ изуча́ют крестья́нский быт. They are studying the peasant life.

при-бы-тие́, arrival — Всего́ час до прибы́тия парохо́да. It's only an hour before the arrival of the boat.

со-бы́-тие, event — В Евро́пе происхо́дят ва́жные собы́тия. Important events are taking place in Europe.

у-бы-ва́ть, to diminish, subside — Вода́ ста́ла убыва́ть. The water began to subside.

B

ВАГ-, WEIGHT, DARE

от-ва́г-а, daring, audacity, hardihood — Го́рцы изве́стны свое́й отва́гой. The mountaineers are known for their daring.

от-ва́ж-ный, daring, courageous

Степа́н отва́жный матро́с. Stephen is a courageous sailor.

от-ва́ж-иться, to dare, venture, risk

Неприя́тель не отва́жится на при́ступ. The enemy will not venture an assault.

ва́ж-ный, important, grave, significant

Это о́чень ва́жный вопро́с. It is a very important question (matter).

ва́ж-ничать, to be proud, to put on airs

Он ва́жничает свои́м чи́ном. He is putting on airs because of his rank.

ва́ж-ность, importance, significance, consequence

Кака́я в э́том ва́жность. It's of no consequence. (What does it matter!)

у-важ-а́ть, to respect, esteem

Вас все уважа́ют. Everybody respects you.

у-важ-е́ние, respect, deference

Мы отно́симся к ней с уваже́нием. We treat her with respect.

у-важ-и́тельный, valid, justifiable, excusable, important

Он не мог зайти́ к вам по уважи́тельной причи́не. He could not call on you for a justifiable reason.

ВАЛ-, ROLL, SURGE, BULWARK, HEAP

вал, rampart, embankment

За ва́лом начина́ются око́пы. The trenches begin beyond the rampart.

вал-и́ть, to throng, to heap, pile, overturn

Наро́д вали́т толпо́й. The people come in a throng.

вал-я́ться, to roll about, loll, to wallow

Он валя́ется в посте́ли до обе́да. He lolls in bed until dinner.

на-по-ва́л, outright, on the spot

Его́ уби́ли напова́л. He was killed outright.

об-ва́л, avalanche, landslide

По́сле землетрясе́ния произоше́л обва́л. After the earthquake there was a landslide.

пере-вал-и́ть, to pass, get across

Ему́ уже́ перевали́ло за шестьдеся́т. He is already past sixty.

про-ва́л-ивать, to reject, send off, chase out

Прова́ливай да́льше! Get along with you! (Get away!)

про-вал-и́ться, to fail, fall through, collapse

Учени́к провали́лся на экза́мене. The student failed in his examination.

раз-ва́л, collapse, disintegration, discord

В их семье́ полне́йший разва́л. In their family everything is at sixes and sevens.

с-ва́л-ка, fight, heap

Ему́ подби́ли глаз в сва́лке. He got a black eye in the fight.

ВАР-, BOIL, HEAT, COOK

вар, tar

Ва́ром поправля́ют доро́ги. The roads are repaired with tar.

вар-е́нье, jam, preserve

Она́ не лю́бит мали́нового варе́нья. She does not like raspberry jam.

вар-и́ть, to cook

Когда́ вы научите́сь вари́ть ка́шу? When will you learn to cook the gruel?

по́-вар, cook

У них по́вар францу́з. Their cook is a Frenchman.

пище-вар-е́ние, digestion

Он страда́ет расстро́йством пищеваре́ния. He suffers from indigestion.

само-ва́р, tea-urn

Самова́р на столе́, пора́ пить чай. The samovar is on the table, it's time to drink tea.

BE-, (ВѢ)- WAFT, BLOW, FAN

ве́-ять, to waft, blow softly

В откры́тое окно́ ве́ет прохла́дой. Cool air blows softly through the open window.

ве́-ялка, winnowing-machine

Ве́ялка в амба́ре. The winnowing-machine is in the barn.

ве́-яние, breeze, influence, idea

Но́вые ве́яния чу́вствуются да́же в прови́нции. New ideas are felt even in the province.

ве́-ер, fan

У неё дорого́й ве́ер. She has an expensive fan.

ве́-тер, wind

Ду́ет си́льный ве́тер. A strong wind blows.

ве́-тряный, wind, windy

На горе́ стои́т ветряна́я ме́льница. There is a windmill on the hill.

вы-ве́-тривать, to weather, to air

Переме́на температу́ры выве́тривает по́чву. A change in temperature weathers the soil.

по-ве́-трие, epidemic, infection

Тепе́рь пове́трие на о́спу. Now there is an epidemic of smallpox.

по-ве́-ять, to begin to blow, flow, spread

В ко́мнате пове́яло за́пахом цвето́в. A fragrance of flowers permeated the room.

про-ве́-тривать, to air

Служа́нка прове́тривает оде́жду. The maid is airing the clothes.

ВЕД-, (ВѢД)-, KNOW
SEE: BET-

вед-ать, to know, be aware

Хозя́ин не ве́дал, что гость не обе́дал. The host did not know that the guest had no dinner.

вед-омость, journal, list, report

Где тамо́женная ве́домость? Where is the customs report?

вед-ьма, witch

Она́ зла как ве́дьма. She is angry as a witch.

веж-ливый, polite

Ве́жливый молодо́й челове́к. A polite young man.

нс-вѐжи а, ignoramus

Непёжка не уме́ет держа́ть себя́ в о́бществе. An ignoramus does not know how to behave in society.

рав-вед-ка, search, exploration, reconnaissance

Мы отпра́вились на разве́дку. We were off to start an exploration.

с-вед-ение, knowledge, information

Они́ не име́ют све́дений о бра́то. They have no information about their brother.

с-вид-е́тель,
(съвѣдѣтель), } witness

Он был свиде́телем э́того преступле́ния. He was a witness in this crime.

ве́-сть(вед-ть), news, message, information

Мы получи́ли прия́тные ве́сти. We received pleasant news.

со́-ве-сть, conscience

Его́ му́чили угрызе́ния со́вести. He was conscience stricken.

добро-со́-ве-стный, conscientious

Он добросо́вестный рабо́тник He is a conscientious worker.

из-ве́-стие, news, information

К нам ре́дко дохо́дят изве́-стия о ней.   We rarely receive news of her.

по́-ве-сть. story, narrative, tale

Я прочёл э́ту по́весть.   I have read this story.

ВЕЛ-, ВОЛ-, COMMAND, WILL, ORDER

вел-е́ть, to order, give orders, command

Вели́ слуге́ принести́ вино́. Give orders to the servant to bring some wine.

по-вел-е́ние, command, order

По высоча́йшему повеле́нию при́говор был отменён. By Imperial order the sentence (verdict) was annulled.

по-вел-и́тель, master, sovereign, commander

На ка́ждого исполни́теля по три повели́теля. For every executive there are three sovereigns (masters).

во́л-я, will, freedom, liberty

Во́ля ва́ша, а я с ва́ми не согла́сен. As you like, but I do not agree with you.

во́л-ь-ный, free, voluntary

Э́то сли́шком во́льный пере-во́д. This translation is too free.

до-во́л-ь-но, enough, suffice, content

Дово́льно говори́ть об э́том. Enough of this talk.

из-во́л-ить, to desire, grant, deign

Чего́ изво́лите?   What do you wish?   (What can I do for you?)

поз-во́л-ить, to allow, permit, let

Позво́льте мне познако́мить вас. Let me introduce you.

удо-во́л-ь-ствие, pleasure, joy, enjoyment

С больши́м удово́льствием. With great pleasure.

вел-ик-а́н, giant

В ци́рке пока́зывали вели-ка́на.   In the circus they were showing a giant.

вел-и́к-ий, great	Наступи́л вели́кий пра́здник Па́схи. There came the great Easter holiday.
вел-ич-а́вый, majestic, stately, lofty	Велича́вый вид Казбе́ка. A majestic view of the Kazbek.
вел-и́ч-ие, grandeur, solemnity	Вели́чие церко́вной слу́жбы. The grandeur of the church service.
вел-ь-мо́жа, courtier	Вельмо́жа прово́дит мно́го вре́мени при дворе́. A courtier spends much time at the court.

ВЕР-, (ВѢР)-, TRUST, FAITH

ве́р-а, faith, religion	Христиа́нская ве́ра распространена́ по всему́ ми́ру. Christianity is spread throughout the world.
ве́р-ить, to trust, believe	Я вам не ве́рю. I do not trust you. (I do not believe you.)
ве́р-ный, faithful	Соба́ка — ве́рный друг челове́ка. The dog is man's faithful friend.
вер-оя́тно, probably, likely	Вы вероя́тно бу́дете здесь за́втра. You will probably be here to-morrow.
до-ве́р-ие, trust, confidence	У меня́ к нему́ по́лное дове́рие. I have complete faith (confidence) in him.
суе-ве́р-ный, superstitious	Суеве́рный всего́ бои́тся. A superstitious person is afraid of everything.
у-ве́р-енность, assurance, certainty	Я не могу́ сказа́ть с уве́ренностью что э́то так. I cannot say with certainty that it is so.

ВЕРТ-, ВРАТ-, ВОРОТ-, TURN, TWIST

верт-е́ть, to turn, twirl, twist

Она́ ве́ртит им как хо́чет. She can twist him around her little finger.

верт-е́ться, to turn round, spin

Сло́во ве́ртится на языке́. The word is on the tip of (my) tongue.

вер-ну́ть(верт-нуть), to return

Он верну́л нам кни́гу. He returned the book to us.

за-вёрт-ывать, } to wrap, roll,
за-вер-ну́ть, } muffle up

Прика́зчик завёртывал (заверну́л) паке́т. The salesman wrapped the parcel.

врат-а́, } gate, gates
воро́т-а, }

Отвори́лись Ца́рские врата́. The holy gates of the sanctuary opened.

вращ-а́ть, to turn, revolve

Стано́к враща́ет колесо́. The lathe turns the wheel.

вращ-а́ться, to revolve, rotate, mix, mingle

Я враща́юсь в образо́ванном о́бществе. I mingle in educated (intellectual) society.

воз-вращ-а́ть, } to return,
воз-врат-и́ть, } pay back

Мы ско́ро возврати́м вам долг. We shall soon return (pay back) our debt to you.

об-ращ-а́ть, to turn, change, convert, transform

Не обраща́йте на него́ внима́ния. Don't pay (turn) any attention to him.

об-рат-и́ть, to turn, change, convert

Обрати́те внима́ние на ва́ши оши́бки. Pay attention to your mistakes.

об-ращ-е́ние, circulation, rotation, usage, treatment

Э́та моне́та вы́шла из обраще́ния. This coin has been out of circulation.

раз-вра́т, corruption, debauch, perversity

Э́то су́щий развра́т. This is a veritable debauch.

раз-врат-ник, libertine, de-praved person — Он превратился в разврат-ника. He turned into a libertine.

раз-вращ-ать, to corrupt — Дурной пример развращает. A bad example corrupts one.

ворот, collar — У него высокий ворот. He wears a high collar.

ворот-а, (врат-а), gate, gates — Ворота открыты настеж. The gates are wide open.

ворот-ить, to return, call back — Прошлого не воротишь. One cannot call back the past.

ворот-ник, collar — Я купил воротники. I bought the collars.

водо-ворот, whirlpool — Лодка попала в водоворот. The boat was caught in a whirlpool.

косо-ворот-ка, Russian shirt — На нём была косоворотка. He wore a Russian shirt.

об-орот (об-ворот), turn — Дело приняло плохой оборот. The affair took a turn for the worse.

пере-ворот, overturn, revolu-tion — В России произошёл пере-ворот. In Russia there was a revolution.

по-ворот, turn, bend, loop, crossroad, return — На повороте мы встретили знакомых. We met (our) acquaintance at the turn in the road.

ВЕРХ-, TOP, ABOVE, SUPER-

верх, top, summit — Верх горы слишком крут. The top of the mountain is too steep.

верх-ний, upper — Мы живём на верхнем этаже. We live on the upper floor.

верх-о́м, horseback, astride | Я люблю́ ката́ться верхо́м. I like horseback riding.

верх-у́шка, top, summit | Мо́лния разби́ла верху́шку де́рева. The lightning smashed the tree top.

верш-и́на, summit, peak | Мы по́днялись на сне́жную верши́ну. We ascended the snow-clad summit.

со-верш-е́нство, perfection | Она́ зна́ет ру́сский язы́к в совершенстве. She knows the Russian language to perfection.

со-верш-и́ть, to perform, commit, accomplish | Он соверши́л преступле́ние. He committed a crime.

ВЕСЕЛ-, JOYFUL, CHEER, ENJOY

весел-и́ть, to cheer, enjoy, amuse | Что кого́ весели́т, тот про то и говори́т. One speaks of those things which one enjoys.

весёл-ый, gay, cheerful | Весёлое лицо́. A cheerful face.

весе́л-ье, joy, gaiety | В до́ме цари́ло весе́лье. Gaiety reigned in the house.

весел-ь-ча́к, merry chap, merrymaker | Мой дя́дя большо́й весельча́к. My uncle is a great merrymaker.

на-весел-е́, tipsy, in one's cups | Вы сего́дня навеселе́. You are tipsy today.

раз-весел-и́ть, to amuse, cheer up | Как вас развесели́ть? How can I cheer you up?

BET-, (ВѢТ)-, UTTER, SAY, SPEAK
SEE: ВЕД-

за-вéт, testament, will, bequest	Храни́те завéты прéдков. Keep the bequest of the ancestors.
о-бéт(об-вет), promise, vow	Онá далá обéт пойти́ в монасты́рь. She has made a vow to enter a convent.
от-вéт, answer, reply	Я ещё не получи́л отвéта. I have not yet received the reply.
при-вéт, greeting	Онá шлёт вам привéт. She sends greetings to you.
со-вéт, advice, counsel	Дáйте емý хорóший совéт. Give him good advice.
со-вéт-чик, adviser, counsellor, guide	Вы плохóй совéтчик. You are a poor adviser.
об-ещ-áть, to promise	Я ничегó не могý вам обещáть. I cannot promise you anything.
от-веч-áть, от-вéт-ить, to answer, reply	Вы ещё не отвéтили на письмó. You have not answered the letter yet.
со-вещ-áться, to confer, consult, deliberate	Они́ дóлго совещáлись. They deliberated a long time.
вéч-е, moot, meeting	Славя́нское вéче бы́ло нарóдным собрáнием. The Slavic moot used to be a popular assembly.

ВИ-, WEAVE

ви-ть, weave, twist, spin	Веснóй пти́цы вьют гнёзда. In spring the birds make their nests.

вь-ю́га, blizzard, snow-storm

На дворе́ во́ет вьюга. The blizzard howls outside.

вь-ю́н, groundling, vine, convolvulus

Он вьётся как вьюн. He twists like a groundling. He clings to one like a vine. (He courts favor by a cringing demeanor.)

вь-ю́чный, burden, pack

Ло́шадь — вью́чное живо́тное. The pack-horse is a beast of burden.

вь-ю́шка, damper, valve

Не забу́дь, откры́ть вьюшку в печи́. Don't forget to open the damper in the stove.

раз-ви́-тие, development

Культу́рное развитие страны́. The cultural development of the country.

раз-ви́-ть, to develop, evolve

Я хочу́ разви́ть э́то де́ло. I want to develop this business.

с-ви́-ть, to wind, coil, wreath, build

Де́вочка сви́ла себе́ вено́к. The little girl has made a wreath for herself.

ВИД-, SEE

вид, view, aspect

Отсю́да прекра́сный вид. The view is beautiful from here.

ви́д-еть, to see

Они́ ви́дят всё в ро́зовом све́те. They see everything through rose-colored glasses.

вид-не́ться, to be seen, appear

Вдали́ видне́ется дере́вня. A village has appeared in the distance.

ви́д-ный, prominent, conspicuous, noticeable

Петро́в занима́ет ви́дное положе́ние. Petrov occupies a prominent place.

воз-не-на-вид-еть, to hate, begin to hate

Она его возненавидела. She began to hate him.

за-вид-овать, to envy, to be envious

Почему вы ему завидуете? Why do you envy him?

за-вис-тливый, envious, jealous

Завистливое око видит далёко. An envious eye sees far.

за́-вис-ть(за-вид-ть), envy, grudge

Её гложет зависть. She is pining away with envy.

при-вид-éние, vision, apparition, ghost

В старину верили в привидéния. In times of yore they believed in ghosts.

с-вид-áние, meeting, appointment

Я спешу на свидание. I am hurrying to an appointment. (I am in a hurry, I have an appointment.)

ВИН-, BLAME

вин-á, blame, fault

Чья это вина? Whose fault is it?

вин-ить, to accuse

Напрасно вы меня вините. You are accusing me unjustly.

вин-овáтый, guilty

Он не признал себя виновáтым. He did not admit that he was guilty.

вин-óвник, culprit, author, cause

Павел сегодня виновник торжества. Paul is the cause of to-day's celebration.

из-вин-éние, pardon, excuse

Прошу извинéния. I beg your pardon. (Excuse me.)

не-вин-ный, innocent, not guilty

Он оказался невинным. He was found innocent.

об-вин-я́ть,
об-вин-и́ть, } to accuse

Их обвиня́ют в кра́же. They are accused of theft.

ВИС-, ВЕС-, (ВѢС)-, HANG

вис-е́ть, to hang

Шу́ба виси́т на ве́шалке. The coat is hanging on a peg.

ви́с-елица, gallows

Его́ приговори́ли к ви́се-лице. He was sentenced to be hanged on the gallows.

за-ви́с-еть, to depend

Э́то от меня́ не зави́сит. It does not depend on me.

вес, weight, importance

Э́то челове́к с ве́сом. He is a man of importance.

вы́-вес-ка, sign

На у́лицах я́ркие вы́вески. There are bright signs on the streets.

за́-на-вес, curtain

За́навес шевели́тся от ве́тра. The curtain is flapping in the wind.

ве́ш-алка, hanger, clothes peg

В пере́дней не́сколько ве́-шалок. There are several hangers in the hall.

ве́ш-ать, to hang

Ба́ба ве́шает бельё на ве-рёвку. The peasant woman hangs the clothes on a rope.

ВЛАД-, POWER, RULE

влад-е́лец, owner

Владе́лец э́того име́ния мой ро́дственник. The owner of this estate is my relative.

влад-е́ние, domain

У него́ обши́рные владе́ния. He has a large domain.

влад-е́ть, to possess, rule, own

А́нглия владе́ет И́ндией. England rules India.

влад-ы́ка, master, owner, ruler

Поме́щик был полновла́ст ным влады́кой крестья́н. The landlord was the absolute master of the peasants.

влáс-твовать, to lord, dominate, rule

Диктáтор влáствует над странóй. A dictator rules the country.

влас-ть(влад-ть), power, authority

Совéтская власть учредúла колхóзы. The Soviet authorities have founded the collective farms.

óб-лас-ть(об-влад-ть), province, region

Примóрская óбласть на берегý Тúхого Океáна. The Maritime province is on the Pacific coast.

ВОД-, WATER

вод-á, water

Дáйте мне стакáн водú. Give me a glass of water.

вóд-ка, vodka

Вóдка крéпкий напúток. Vodka is a hard liquor.

вод-о-вóз, water carrier

Водовóз проéхал по ýлице. The water carrier passed along the street.

вод-о-пáд, waterfall, falls

Ниагáрский водопáд великолéпен. The Niagara Falls are magnificent.

вод-о-про-вóд, water-pipe, plumbing

У нас испóртился водопровóд. Our plumbing is out of order.

на-вод-нéние, flood

Наводнéние причиняет мнóго бéдствий. A flood causes many hardships.

под-вóд-ный, submarine, subaqueous

Подвóдная лóдка пошлá ко днý. The submarine sank.

ВОД-, ВЕД-, LEAD

вод-úть, to lead

Мáльчик вóдит слепóго зá руку. The boy leads the blind man by the hand.

вожд-ь, leader	Ле́нин был вождём пролета́риа́та. Lenin was the leader of the proletariat.
вы́-вод, conclusion	Я заключи́л неблагоприя́тный вы́вод. I have made an unfavorable conclusion.
пере-во́д, translation	Э́та кни́га — перево́д с ру́сского. This book is a translation from the Russian.
по́-вод, ground, reason, cause	Война́ загоре́лась без вся́кого по́вода. The war broke out for no reason.
рав-во́д, divorce	Он уже́ получи́л разво́д. He has already been granted a divorce.
вес-ти́ (вед-ти), to lead, conduct, manage	Не легко́ вести́ тако́е большо́е де́ло. It is not easy to manage such a big business.
в-вед-е́ние, introduction	Ва́ше введе́ние сли́шком кра́тко. Your introduction is too brief.
ва-вед-е́ние, institution	Я учу́сь в вы́сшем уче́бном заведе́нии. I am studying in an institution of higher learning.
ва-вес-ти́, to lead, bring, take	Вы завели́ меня́ далеко́ в парк. You led me too far into the park.
от-вес-ти́, to take	Я отведу́ её домо́й. I shall take her home.
по-вед-е́ние, demeanor, conduct	Ученика́ наказа́ли за дурно́е поведе́ние. The pupil was punished for misdemeanor.
про-из-вед-е́ние, work, writing	Она́ прочла́ все произве-де́ния Толсто́го. She has read all the works of Tolstoy.

про-из-вод-и́ть, } to make
про-из-вес-ти́, }

Эта пье́са произвела́ на меня́ хоро́шее впечатле́ние. This play made a good impression on me.

ВОЗ-, ВЕЗ-, CARRY

вез-ти́, } to take, carry,
воз-и́ть, } bring

Крестья́нин везёт гусе́й на я́рмарку. The peasant brings the geese to the fair.

воз, cart

Мужи́к про́дал воз се́на. The peasant sold a cartload of hay.

воз-ня́, racket, noise

Что э́то там за возня́? What is that racket?

вы-воз-и́ть, to export

Росси́я вывозит хлеб заграни́цу. Russia exports grain (abroad).

из-во́з-чик, cabman

Позови́те изво́зчика. Call a cabman.

паро-во́з, engine, locomotive

Около ста́нции показа́лся парово́з. An engine appeared at the station.

пере-во́з, transport, transportation

Фи́рма уплати́ла за перево́з това́ра. The concern paid for the transportation of goods.

ВОЛОК-, ВЛЕК-, ВЛАК-, PULL, DRAG, FIBRE

волок-и́та, dangler

Он ста́рый волоки́та. He is an old dangler.

волок-но́, fibre

Это льняно́е волокно́ для пря́жи. This linen fibre is for weaving.

на́-волок-а, pillowcase

Принеси́те мне чи́стую на́волоку. Bring me a clean pillowcase.

про́-волок-а, wire

На столбе́ виси́т про́волока. A wire is hanging on the pole.

волоч-и́ть, to drag

От уста́лости я едва́ волочи́л но́ги. I could hardly drag my feet because of weariness.

волоч-и́ться, to run after

Офице́ры волочи́лись ва ней. The officers were running after her.

влеч-е́ние, inclination, proclivity

У меня́ большо́е влече́ние к му́зыке. I have a proclivity to music.

влеч-ь (влек-ть), to bring, involve

Э́то влечёт ва собо́ю непри-я́тности. It may bring annoyance.

при-влек-а́ть, to attract, summon, prosecute

Его́ привлека́ют к отве́тст-венности. He is being prosecuted.

рав-влек-а́ть, to amuse, entertain

И́гры развлека́ют дете́й. Games amuse children.

у-влек-а́ть, to attract, fascinate

Их увлека́ет теа́тр. The theatre fascinates them.

влач-и́ть, to drag, lead

Он влачи́т жа́лкое суще-ствова́ние. He leads a wretched existence.

о́б-лак-о (об-влак-о), cloud

Не́бо покры́то облака́ми. The sky is overcast.

ВЫС-, HIGH

выс-о́кий, high, tall

Како́е высо́кое зда́ние. What a high building.

выс-окоме́рие, haughtiness, arrogance

Его́ презира́ли ва высоко-ме́рие. He was despised for his arrogance.

выс-ок-опáрный, pompous

Статьá напи́сана высоко-
пáрным слóгом. The arti-
cle is written in a pompous
style.

выс-отá, height, altitude

Он оказáлся на высотé
положéния. He rose to
the occasion.

выс-ь, height

Жáворонок лети́т в высь.
The lark soars upwards.

воз-выш-áть,) to raise,
воз-вы́с-ить,) promote

Егó возвы́сили до генерáль-
ского чи́на. He was pro-
moted to the rank of
general.

воз-выш-éние, elevation

На возвышéнии стои́т крé-
пость. There is a fortress
on the elevation.

по-выш-éние, promotion

Он получи́л повышéние. He
received a promotion.

ВЯЗ-, УЗ-, TIE, BIND

вяз-анка, bundle

Он принёс вя́занку дров.
He brought a bundle of
wood.

вяз-áть, to knit

Вы́учи меня́ вязáть чулки́.
Teach me how to knit
stockings.

вя́з-нуть, to stick

В дождь мы вя́знем в грязи́.
When it rains, we stick in
the mud.

вяз-ь, ornamental lettering

Письмó напи́сано славя́нской
вя́зью. The document is
written in Slavic orna-
mental lettering.

за-вя́з-ка, plot

Завя́зка ромáна интерéсна.
The plot of the novel is
interesting.

об-яз-а́тельство, promise, pledge

Я взял с него́ пи́сьменное обяза́тельство. I took a written pledge from him.

об-я́з-ывать, (об-вяз-ывать), to bind legally, oblige

Э́то ни к чему́ не обя́зывает. There is nothing binding in that.

раз-вя́з-ка, climax

Де́ло идёт к развя́зке. The affair is coming to a head.

у́в-ел, knot

Она́ завяза́ла у́зел на платке́. She tied a knot in her handkerchief.

у́в-ник, prisoner

У́зника сего́дня освободи́ли. The prisoner was released today.

у́в-ы, ties

Его́ тяготя́т у́зы родства́. He is weary of his family ties.

Г

ГАД-, GUESS

гад-а́лка, fortuneteller

Тётя была́ у гада́лки. Our aunt was at the fortune-teller's.

гад-а́ть, to tell fortunes

В старину́ ча́сто гада́ли. In old days they often told fortunes.

гад-а́ние, fortunetelling, divination

Она́ ве́рила в гада́ние. She believed in fortunetelling.

до-га́д-ываться, } to guess
до-гад-а́ться,

Я сам догада́лся что он музыка́нт. I myself guessed that he was a musician.

до-га́д-ка, conjecture, guess

Пошли́ ра́зные дога́дки. Various conjectures were abroad.

за-га́д-ка, riddle

Отгада́йте э́ту зага́дку. Guess this riddle.

за-га́д-очный, mysterious

Кака́я зага́дочная исто́рия. What a mysterious incident.

у-гад-а́ть, to guess

Угада́йте от кого́ цветы́. Guess from whom are these flowers.

ГАД-, REPTILE

гад, reptile

В тропи́ческих стра́нах мно́го вся́ких га́дов. In tropical countries there are all kinds of reptiles.

га́д-кий, mean, base

Вы соверши́ли га́дкий посту́пок. You have done a mean trick.

га́д-ость, baseness, meanness

Он спосо́бен на вся́кие га́дости. He is capable of all sorts of meanness.

ГИБ-, ГН-, ГУБ-, PERIL, BEND, BOW

ги́б-ель, destruction, peril

Мы бы́ли на краю́ ги́бели. We were on the verge of destruction.

ги́б-кий, flexible, pliable, willowy

У меня́ в рука́х ги́бкий прут. I hold a willowy rod.

ги́б-кость, suppleness, subtlety

Он отлича́ется ги́бкостью ума́. He is noted for his subtlety.

ги́б-нуть, to perish

Мно́гие ги́бнут в тюрьма́х. Many perish in prisons.

гн-уть (гбн-уть), to bend

Крестья́нин гнёт спи́ну всю жизнь. The peasant works hard all his life.

из-ги́б, curve, bent

По э́той доро́ге мно́го изги́бов. There are many curves along this road.

на-гн-у́ться, to bend, stoop	Мать нагну́лась к ребёнку. The mother bent down to her child.
по-ги́б-ель, destruction, peril, undoing	Э́то бы́ло его́ поги́белью. This was his undoing.
с-ги́б-а́ть, to bend	Рабо́тник сгиба́ет дугу́. The laborer is bending a bow.
со-гн-у́ть, to bend, twist, curve	Сталь мо́жно согну́ть не ломая. One may bend the steel without breaking it.
губ-и́тель, destroyer, undoer	Он настоя́щий губи́тель серде́ц. He is a veritable lady-killer.
губ-и́ть, to ruin, destroy, kill	Моро́з гу́бит жа́тву. Frost kills the crop.
по-губ-и́ть, to ruin, undo	Его́ погуби́ла пра́здность. Idleness ruined him.

ГЛАВ-, ГОЛОВ-, HEAD, CHIEF

глав-а́, head, chief, principal, chapter	Его́ брат глава́ фи́рмы. His brother is the head of the firm.
	Мы прочли́ пе́рвую главу́. We have read the first chapter.
гла́в-ный, chief, main, primary	Гла́вной те́мой разгово́ра была́ война́. War was the main topic of conversation.
за-гла́в-ие, heading, title	Загла́вие кни́ги сли́шком дли́нно. The title of the book is too long.
о-глав-ле́ние, table of contents, index	Посмотри́те в оглавле́ние. Look into the table of contents.

голов-а́, head

У меня́ боли́т голова́. I have a headache.

голов-о-круже́ние, dizziness

Она́ страда́ет головокруже́нием. She suffers from dizziness. She has dizzy spells.

голов-о-ло́мный,   puzzling, difficult to solve

Учи́тель за́дал головоло́мную зада́чу. The teacher gave a braintwister. The teacher gave a difficult problem.

из-голо́в-ие, head of the bed

О́браз виси́т у изголо́вья. An ikon hangs at the head of the bed.

ГЛАД-, SMOOTH, PAT

гла́д-ить, to iron, press

Сестра́ гла́дит платки́. My sister irons the handkerchiefs.

гла́д-кий, smooth, even

Лёд на реке́ гла́дкий как стекло́. The ice on the river is as smooth as glass.

глад-ь, smooth surface, stillness

Кака́я гладь на́ море сего́дня. How smooth the sea is today.

за-гла́ж-ивать, to smooth, efface, expiate, make up, make amends

Он загла́живает свою́ вину́. He is making amends for his fault.

раз-гла́ж-ивать, }to smooth
раз-гла́д-ить,   }

Де́вочка разгла́дила измя́тое пла́тье. The little girl smoothed out a crumpled dress.

ГЛАД-, ГОЛОД-, HUNGER

глод-а́ть, to gnaw, nibble

Соба́ка гло́жет кость. The dog gnaws the bone.

го́лод, hunger, famine

В э́той стране́ свире́пствовал го́лод. Famine ravaged (in) this country.

голод-а́ть, to starve, to be hungry

Безрабо́тные голода́ют. The unemployed are starving.

голо́д-ный, hungry

Послы́шался вой голо́дного во́лка. The howl of a hungry wolf was heard.

про-голод-а́ться, to be hungry

Я о́чень проголода́лась. I am very hungry.

ГЛАЗ-, EYE

глаз, eye

У неё прекра́сные глаза́. She has beautiful eyes.

глаз-е́ть, to stare

Толпа́ зева́к глазе́ла на аэропла́н. A crowd of idlers stared at the airplane.

гла́з-ки, eyes

Не́чего вам стро́ить гла́зки. You must not make eyes (at me).

глаз-но́й, eye

Мне на́до пойти́ к глазно́му врачу́. I have to go to an oculist.

за-глаз-а́, behind one's back, amply

Про кого́ не говоря́т за-глаза́? Is there anyone of whom they don't talk behind his back?

с-гла́з-ить, to cast an evil spell

Крестья́нка говори́т что её ребёнка сгла́зили. The peasant woman says that someone has cast an evil spell on her child.

ГЛАС-, ГОЛОС-, VOICE

глас, voice, tune

Глас наро́да, глас Бо́жий. The voice of the people is the voice of God.

глас-и́ть, to say, run, go

Так гласи́т статья́ зако́на. It is said so in the legal statute.

глáс-ный, vowel, public	Ученикú произнóсят глáсные звýки. The pupils are pronouncing the vowel sounds.
глаш-áтай, town-crier	Глашáтаи бы́стро разнеслú весть. The town-criers spread the news swiftly.
при-глаш-áть, при-глас-úть, } to invite	Пригласúте их на чай. Invite them to tea.
при-глаш-éние, invitátion	Мы получúли приглашéние на бал. We have received the invitation to the ball.
со-глáс-ие, consent, agreement	Он не хóчет дать своегó соглáсия. He does not want to give his consent.
со-глаш-áться, со-глас-úться, } to agree	Я согласúлся поéхать с нúми. I agreed to go with them.
вóз-глас, ejaculation, outcry	Послы́шались вóзгласы и восклицáния. There were heard ejaculations and exclamations.
едино-глáс-но, unanimous-ly	Резолю́цию прúняли единоглáсно. The resolution was unanimously passed.
о-глáс-ка, publicity	Это извéстие не подлежúт оглáске. This information is not to be made public. (is not to be broadcast).
гóлос, voice	У Шаля́пина великолéпный гóлос. Shaliapin has a magnificent voice.
голос-úстый, loud-voiced, vociferous	В лесý раздавáлось пéние голосúстых птиц. A loud singing of the birds resounded in the forest.

голос-ова́ть, to vote — Мно́гие голосова́ли про́тив э́того кандида́та. Many voted against this candidate.

ГЛУХ-, ГЛОХ-, DEAF

глух-о́й, deaf — Глухо́му с немы́м не́чего говори́ть. It's no use for the deaf to talk with the dumb.

глух-о-немо́й, deaf-mute — На углу́ дом для глухо-немы́х. On the corner there is a home for deaf-mutes.

глуш-и́ть, to deafen — Гроза́ нередко глу́шит людей. Thunder frequently deafens people.

глуш-ь, solitary, remote place — Они́ живу́т в глуши́. They live in a remote place.

о-глуш-а́ть, } o-глуш-и́ть, } to deafen, stun — Пу́шечный вы́стрел оглуши́л меня́. The gunfire deafened me.

гло́х-нуть, to grow deaf — Он стал гло́хнуть. He began to get hard of hearing.

о-гло́х-нуть, to become deaf — Ба́бушка огло́хла. The grandmother became deaf.

ГЛЯД-, GLANCE, LOOK

гляд-е́ть, to look, glance — Он гляде́л на меня́ в упо́р. He stared at me.

вы́-гляд-еть, to look — Вы хорошо́ вы́глядите. You look well.

за-гля́д-ывать, to look in, peep in — Не загля́дывайте в кни́гу. Don't look in your book.

за-гля-ну́ть(за-гляд-нуть), to call, drop in

Загляни́те к нам ве́чером. Come to see (Call on) us tonight.

о-гля́д-ываться, ⎫ to look back, look round, turn round
о-гля-ну́ться, ⎭

Она́ ча́сто огля́дывается. She often looks back.

Не успе́ли огляну́тся как ле́то прошло́. We had hardly turned round when the summer was gone.

вз-гляд, look, view, outlook, opinion

У вас здра́вый взгляд на ве́щи. You have a sound judgment (outlook).

о-гля́д-ка, looking back

Он бежа́л без огля́дки. He ran without looking back (turning his head).

ГН-, ГОН-, CHASE, DRIVE

гн-ать, ⎫ to chase, drive, spur on, bucket, drive, chase
гон-я́ть, ⎭

Изво́зчик го́нит ло́шадь. The cabman buckets his horse.

Де́вушка гоня́ет кур с огоро́да. The girl chases the chickens out of the truck-garden.

гон-е́ние, persecution, oppression

Раско́льники подверга́лись гоне́нию. The dissenters were subjected to persecution.

го́н-ка, race, regatta

За́втра состои́тся гребна́я го́нка. The regatta will be tomorrow.

вы́-гн-ать, to drive out, turn out

Хозя́ин вы́гнал прика́зчика. The boss has turned out the clerk.

до-гон-я́ть, ⎫ to catch up, overtake
до-гн-а́ть, ⎭

Вы иди́те, я вас догоню́. Go, I will catch up with you.

из-гн-а́ние, exile

За свои́ убежде́ния он жил в изгна́нии. For his convictions he lived in exile.

обо-гн-а́ть, to leave behind, outdistance, pass by

Нас обогна́л автомоби́ль. An automobile passed us by.

по-го́н-я, chase, pursuit

В пого́не за деньга́ми Заха́ров потеря́л здоро́вье. In his pursuit of money Zakharov has lost his health.

ГНЕВ-, (ГНѢВ)-, ANGER

гнев, anger

В припа́дке гне́ва писа́тель уничто́жил ру́копись. In a paroxysm of anger the writer has destroyed his manuscript.

гне́в-аться, to be angry, to fume

Нача́льник напра́сно гне́вался. The chief was angry for nothing.

гне́в-ный, angry

Муж бро́сил гне́вный взгляд на жену́. The husband looked angrily at his wife.

ГНЕТ-, PRESS

гнес-ти́ (гнет-ти), to oppress

Меня́ гнетёт нужда́. Poverty oppresses me.

гнёт, oppression

Наро́д изнемога́ет под гнётом ра́бства. The people are exhausted under the oppression of slavery.

у-гнет-а́ть, to oppress

Заво́дчик угнета́ет рабо́чих. The factory owner oppresses his workers.

у-гнет-ённый, oppressed, depressed

Я заста́л дру́га в угнетённом состоя́нии. I found my friend very depressed.

ГНИ-, ГНОЙ-, ROT

гни-лóй, rotten, foul	Тут пáхнет гнилóй рыбой. There is a smell of rotten fish here.
гни-ть, to rot, decay	Сéно гниёт от сырости. The hay rots in the dampness.
с-гни-вáть, to rot, decay	Кóрень дéрева сгнивáет. The root of the tree is decaying.
гной, pus, matter	Из рáны сочится гной. The wound is festering.

ГОВОР-, TALK

гóвор, talk, conversation	На улице слышен гóвор. Talking is heard in the street.
говор-úть, to speak, talk	Мы говорúм по-рýсски. We speak Russian
говор-ýн, chatterer, chatter-box	Этот студéнт стрáшный гово-рýн. This student is a veritable chatterbox.
вы-говор, reprimand, rebuke, pronunciation	Отéц сдéлал выговор сыну. The father reprimanded his son.
дó-говор, treaty, agreement	Дóговор подпúсан. The treaty is signed.
зá-говор, plot, conspiracy	Зáговор раскрыт. The plot is discovered.
за-говóр-щик, conspirator	Заговóрщика поймáли. They caught the conspirator.
от-говóр-ка, excuse, pretext	Вы не отдéлаетесь отговóр-ками. You cannot get away with (your) excuses.
по-говóр-ка, saying, adage, proverb	Рýсский язык богáт поговóр-ками. The Russian lan-guage is rich in adages.

раз-говóр, talk, conversation

В гости́ной шёл оживлённый разговóр. In the drawing-room there was animated talk.

у-говóр, agreement, understanding

Такóв был наш уговóр. Such was our understanding.

с-говор-и́ться, to agree, make arrangement

Мы наконéц сговори́лись. Finally we agreed upon it. (Finally we made the arrangements.)

ГОД-, YEAR, TIME, WEATHER, FIT, GOOD

год, year

В э́том годý рáнняя веснá. The spring is early this year.

год-овóй, yearly, annual

Купéц подсчи́тывал годовóй дохóд. The merchant was figuring out the yearly profit.

год-овщи́на, anniversary

В годовщи́ну смéрти Пýшкина устрóили концéрт. On the anniversary of Pushkin's death they had a concert.

по-гóд-а, weather

Сегóдня прекрáсная погóда. The weather is beautiful today.

год-и́ться, to suit, fit, do

Ваш словáрь мне не годи́тся. Your dictionary won't do.

гóд-ный, fit, suitable

Э́та минерáльная водá годнá для питья́. This mineral water is fit (good) for drinking.

вы́-год-а, profit, gain, advantage, benefit

Нáше изобрéтение принóсит нам вы́году. Our invention brings us profit.

у-гожд-а́ть,⎫
⎪ to please,
⎬ gratify
у-год-и́ть, ⎭

На весь свет не угоди́шь.
You cannot please the en-
tire world.

На всех и со́лнце не уго-
жда́ет. Even the sun
cannot please everybody.

ГОЛ-, NAKED

го́л-ый, naked, bare

Мы спа́ли на го́лой земле́.
We slept on the bare
ground.

гол-ь, bareness, poverty, poor
people

Голь на вы́думки хитра́.
Necessity is the mother of
invention.

гол-о-ле́дица, sleet, rime

На дворе́ стоя́ла гололе́дица.
Outside the ground was
covered with ice.

ГОР-, ГРЕ-, HILL, MOUNT, HEAT, BURN, BITTER,
WOE

гор-а́, mountain

Вдали́ видне́ется крута́я
гора́. A steep mountain is
seen in the distance.

гор-носта́й, ermine

Горноста́й це́нное живо́тное.
The ermine is a valuable
animal.

го́р-ный, mountainous, mountain

Го́рные ручьи́ быстры́. The
mountain streams are rapid.

го́р-ничная, maid

Го́рничная мете́т пол. The
maid is sweeping the floor.

при-го́р-ок, hillock

На приго́рке берёзовая ро́ща.
On the hillock there is a
grove of birches.

гор-е́ть, to burn

Ого́нь в камине́ гори́т я́рко.
The fire in the fireplace
burns brightly.

гор-я́чий, hot

Да́йте мне стака́н горя́чего ча́ю. Let me have a glass of hot tea.

гор-я́чка, high fever

Наш знако́мый заболе́л горя́чкой. Our friend (acquaintance) has been stricken with a high fever.

до-гор-а́ть, to burn low, burn out

Костёр догора́ет. The bonfire is burning low.

раз-га́р, heat, climax, full swing

Бал был в по́лном разга́ре. The ball was in full swing.

раз-гор-е́ться, to blaze, get hot

Щёки разгоре́лись от волне́ния. (His) cheeks blazed with excitement.

у-га́р, smoke, fume

От уга́ра разболе́лась голова́. The fumes gave me a headache.

у-гор-е́лый, frenzied, like a madman, as if possessed

Он вы́скочил и́з дому как угоре́лый. He rushed out of the house like a madman.

гре-ть, to warm, heat

Ма́льчик гре́ет ру́ки у пе́чки. The boy warms his hands at the stove.

под-о-гре́-ть, to warm up

Пора́ подогре́ть у́жин. It's time to warm up the supper.

со-гре́-ться, to get warm

Я ника́к не могу́ согре́ться. I simply cannot get warm.

го́р-е, grief, sorrow, misfortune

Слеза́ми го́рю не помо́жешь. There is no use crying over spilt milk. (Tears won't help one in sorrow.)

гор-ева́ть, to grieve, mourn

Она́ горю́ет по поко́йной ма́тери. She mourns for her dead mother.

гор-емы́чный, wretched, miserable

Житьё на́ше горемы́чное. Our wretched existence (life).

гóр-ечь, bitter taste, bitter-ness

У меня горечь во рту. I have a bitter taste in my mouth.

гóр-ь-кий, bitter

Хрен горек на вкус. The horse-radish tastes bitter.

гор-чица, mustard

Я не ем горчицы. I don't eat mustard.

о-гор-чать, to distress, vex

Не огорчай стариков. Don't vex the old people.

о-гор-чéние, regret, concern, distress, sorrow, affliction

С глубоким огорчéнием мы узнали о вашей потéре. With deep regret we have learned of your bereavement.

ГÓРЛ-, THROAT

гóрл-о, throat

У неё болит горло. She has a sore throat.

горл-áнить, to brawl, roar, vociferate

Толпа пьяных горланит. The drunken crowd is roaring.

горл-овóй, throat

У него горловáя болéзнь. He has a throat ailment.

о-жерéл-ье(о-герел-ие), neck-lace

На ней дорогóе ожерéлье. She wears an expensive necklace.

ГОТÓВ-, READY

готóв-ить, to prepare, make ready

На кухне готóвят обéд. In the kitchen they are preparing the dinner.

готóв-ый, ready

Я готóв, пойдёмте. I am ready, let's go.

за-готóв-ительный, supply-ing, purveying

Заготовительный комитéт заседáет. The purveying committee is holding a conference.

на-гото́в-е, prepared, in readiness, to be on the lookout

Бу́дьте нагото́ве. Be prepared. (Be on the lookout.)

под-гото́в-ка, preparation

Студе́нты за́няты подгото́вкой к экза́менам. The students are preparing (studying) for (their) examinations.

при-готов-ля́ть, }
при-гото́в-ить, } to prepare

Брат приготовля́ет уро́к. (My) brother is preparing his lesson.

ГРАД-, ГОРОД-, TOWN, ENCLOSURE

го́род, city, town

Москва́ столи́чный го́род. Moscow is the capital city.

город-ово́й, policeman

Городово́й стои́т на углу́ у́лицы. A policeman stands on the street corner.

город-ско́й, municipal, public

В городско́м саду́ игра́ла му́зыка. A band played in the municipal garden.

горож-а́нин, city dweller

Горожа́не ма́ло знако́мы с се́льским бы́том. City dwellers are little familiar with village customs (life).

о-горо́д, vegetable garden, truck garden

Вокру́г огоро́да была́ изгородь. There was a fence around the vegetable garden.

пере-горо́д-ка, partition

За перегоро́дкой стоя́ла крова́ть. Behind the partition there was a bed.

гражд-ани́н, citizen

Граждани́н Ло́мов произно́сит речь. Citizen Lomov is making a speech.

гражд-а́нство, citizenship

Он получи́л пра́во гражда́нства. He was admitted to citizenship.

о-гра́д-а, fence, wall

У кла́дбища нет никако́й огра́ды. The cemetery is not fenced.

пре-гра́д-а, barrier, hindrance, obstacle

Воображе́ние прегра́д не зна́ет. Imagination knows no obstacles.

ГРЕБ-, ГРАБ-, ГРОБ-, DIG, GRAB

гре́б-ень, comb

Ей ну́жен гре́бень. She needs a comb.

грес-ти́ (греб-ти), to row

Греби́те к бе́регу. Row towards the shore.

вы-греб-а́ть, to rake out

Я выгреба́ю золу́ из печи́. I am raking the ashes out of the stove.

по-греб-а́ть, to bury

Крестья́не ча́сто погреба́ют де́ньги. Often the peasants bury their money.

граб-ёж, robbery, holdup

Грабёж среди́ бе́ла дня. A holdup in broad daylight.

гра́б-ить, о-гра́б-ить, } to rob

Их вчера́ огра́били. They were robbed yesterday.

гра́б-ли, rake

Садо́вник принёс гра́бли. The gardener brought the rake.

гроб, coffin

В це́ркви стои́т чёрный гроб. There is a black coffin in the church.

гроб-овщи́к, coffin maker

Чита́ли-ли вы расска́з о гробовщике́? Have you read the story about the coffin maker?

гроб-ни́ца, tomb

Ви́дели-ли вы гробни́цу Вашингто́на? Did you see Washington's tomb?

за-гроб-ный, sepulchral, hollow, beyond the grave

Он произнёс это загробным голосом. He said this in a sepulchral voice.

ГРЕМ-, ГРОМ-, THUNDER, ROAR

грем-еть, to roar, rumble

За холмом гремят пушки. The guns rumble beyond the hill.

грем-учий, rattle, ring

Мы видели гремучую змею. We saw a rattlesnake.

по-грем-ушка, rattle

Ребёнок забавляется погремушкой. The child plays with a rattle.

гром, thunder

Гром грянул и пошёл дождь. A thunder-clap was heard, and it began to rain.

гром-ить, to ruin, destroy

Войска громили неприятеля. The troops were destroying the enemy.

гром-кий, loud

Она заговорила громким голосом. She spoke loudly. (She spoke in a loud voice.)

гром-о-отвод, lightning-rod

На крыше громоотвод. There is a lightning-rod on the roof.

по-гром, pogrom, massacre, devastation

Во время погрома убили его дядю. His uncle was killed during the pogrom.

раз-гром, destruction, havoc

В канцелярии полнейший разгром. There is complete havoc in the office.

ГРЕХ-, (ГРѢХ)-, SIN

грех, sin, transgression, fault

Не вспоминай грехов юности моей. Don't dwell (remind me of) upon the sins of my youth.

греш-и́ть, to sin, do wrong

> Уме́й греши́ть, уме́й и ка́яться. If you know how to sin, you must know how to repent.

гре́ш-ный, sinful

> Гре́шный челове́к, пью. I drink, sinful man that I am.

по-гре́ш-ность, error, mistake

> В стати́стике погре́шность неизбе́жна. In statistics errors are unavoidable.

ГРОЗ-, AWE, THREAT, ROAR

гроз-а́, thunderstorm

> Гро́зы у нас быва́ют ча́сто. We have frequent thunderstorms.

гроз-и́ть, to threaten, brandish

> Матро́с грози́л кулако́м. The sailor brandished his fist.

гро́з-ный, threatening, menacing, terrible

> Он гро́зно посмотре́л на меня́. He looked menacingly at me.

у-гро́з-а, threat, menace

> Ва́ши угро́зы меня́ не страша́т. Your threats do not frighten me.

у-грож-а́ть, to threaten, menace

> Он угрожа́ет что он уе́дет. He threatens that he will leave.

ГРУБ-, COARSE

груб-ия́н, rude fellow, ruffian

> Како́й-то грубия́н толкну́л её. A ruffian pushed her.

гру́б-ость, rudeness, coarseness

> Его́ не те́рпят за гру́бость. He is not tolerated for his rudeness.

гру́б-ый, rude, coarse

> У дикаре́й гру́бые нра́вы. The savages have rude customs.

о-груб-еть, to become coarse, callous

Он огрубе́л живя́ на да́льнем се́вере. Living in the far north, he became **coarse**.

ГРУЗ-, WEIGHT

груз, freight, cargo, load

Мы получи́ли большо́й груз. We received a large **cargo**.

груз-о-ви́к, truck

Грузовики́ отпра́влены в Росси́ю. The **trucks** were sent to Russia.

на-груж-а́ть, to load

Уже́ нагружа́ют парохо́д. They are already **loading** the steamer.

ГУЛ-, STROLL

гул-я́ние, promenade, walk

Сёстры пошли́ на гуля́ние. The sisters went for a **walk** on the promenade.

гул-я́ть, to walk

Ня́ня гуля́ет с детьми́. The nurse **walks** with the children.

про-гу́л-иваться, to saunter, walk

Они́ прогу́ливаются по на́бе-режной. They are **saunter**-ing along the quay.

про-гу́л-ка, hike, picnic

Дава́йте устро́им прогу́лку. Let's have a **picnic**.

раз-гу́л, revelry, riot

В каза́рме пья́ный разгу́л. There was a drunken **riot** in the barracks.

ГУСТ-, THICK

густ-е́ть, to thicken

Варе́нье густе́ет. The jam is getting **thick** (syrupy).

густ-о́й, thick, dense

Мы забра́лись в густо́й лес. We came into a **dense** forest.

густ-отá, density, thickness

По густотé населéния áтот гóрод на пéрвом мéсте. In density of population this city ranks first.

гýщ-а, dregs, grounds

Онá вы́бросила кофéйную гýщу. She threw out the coffee grounds.

Д

ДА-, GIVE

да-нь, tribute, contribution

Рýсские дóлго платúли дань татáрам. For a long time the Russians paid tribute to the Tartars.

дá-тельный, dative

Окончáние дáтельного падежá легкó запóмнить. It is easy to remember the ending of the dative case.

да-ть, to give

Мне нéчего вам дать. (I can give you nothing.) I have nothing to give you.

воз-да-вáть, to reward, render, return

Есть лю́ди, котóрые воздаю́т добрóм за зло. There are people who render good for evil.

вы́-да-ча, distribution, giving out

На пóчте вы́дача пúсем до пятú часóв. At the post-office the letters are given out until five o'clock.

за-дá-ча, problem, question

Трýдно решúть áту задáчу. It is difficult to solve this problem.

от-да-вáть,
от-дá-ть,
} to give, render, return

Солдáт отдаёт честь полкóвнику. The soldier (returns a salute) salutes the colonel.

Нáдо отдáть емý дóлжное. One must render him his due.

по-да-ва́ть, to present, serve	Официа́нт подаёт ку́шанье. The waiter serves the food.
по-да́-тель, bearer	Пода́тель э́того письма́ мой хоро́ший знако́мый. The bearer of this letter is a good friend of mine.
по-да-я́ние, charity, alms	Ни́щий проси́л подая́ние. The beggar asked for alms.
по́д-да-нный, subject, citizen	Я америка́нский по́дданный. I am an American citizen.
пре́-да-нность, loyalty, devotion	Он изве́стен свое́й пре́данностью де́лу. He is known for his devotion to the cause.
при-да́-ное, dowry	Неве́ста получи́ла бога́тое прида́ное. The bride got a rich dowry.
про-да-ва́ть, про-да́-ть, } to sell	На́ша ба́бушка продала́ име́ние. Our grandmother sold her estate.
рас-про-да́-жа, sale	В магази́не за́втра больша́я распрода́жа. Tomorrow there will be a big sale in the store.
с-да́-ча, change	Я уже́ получи́ла сда́чу. I have already received the change.
у-да́-ча, success, good luck	Жела́ю вам уда́чи. I wish you success. (I wish you good luck.)
да-р, gift, present	Тала́нт — дар с не́ба. Talent is a gift from heaven.
да-рова́ние, gift, talent, endowment	У него́ музыка́льное дарова́ние. He has a talent for music.

да́-ром, nothing, gratis

Мне э́то и да́ром не на́до. I don't want this even for nothing.

бла́го-да-ри́ть, to thank

Благодарю́ вас за любе́зность. I thank you for your kindness.

по-да-ри́ть, to give, make a present

Подари́те мне э́ту кни́гу. Give me this book as a present.

по-да́р-ок, present

Я пода́рков не даю́. I do not give presents.

ДАВ-, FORMER, OLD, PRESS, CRUSH

да́в-ний, long, old

Мы зна́комы с да́вних пор. We have known each other for a long time.

дав-но́, long

Давно́-ли вы здесь? How long have you been here?

да́в-ность, remoteness, antiquity, long lapse of time

По да́вности я не по́мню э́того происше́ствия. Because of a lapse of time I do not remember this accident.

из-да́в-на, long ago, long since

Этот поря́док заведён из-да́вна. This order was established long ago.

не-да́в-но, recently

Неда́вно здесь был пожа́р. There was a fire here recently.

дав-и́ть, to press, oppress, hurt

У меня́ да́вит грудь. My chest hurts.

да́в-ка, crowd, press, jam

В да́вке я потеря́л кошелёк. I have lost my purse in the crowd.

дав-ле́ние, pressure

Баро́метр осно́ван на возду́шном давле́нии. The barometer is based on the atmospheric pressure.

за-дав-и́ть, to run over, crush

Кого́-то задави́ли автомо-
би́лем. Somebody was
crushed by an automobile.

ДВ-, TWO

дв-а, two

Одолжи́те мне два рубля́.
Lend me two roubles.

дв-а́жды, twice

Два́жды два — четы́ре.
Twice two is four.

дв-ена́дцать, twelve

В году́ двена́дцать ме́сяцев.
There are twelve months in
a year.

дв-о́е, two

Нас бы́ло дво́е. There were
two of us.

дв-о́йка, two, two marks,
pair

Учени́к получи́л дво́йку. The
pupil got the grade of two.

дв-ойни́к, double

Он мой двойни́к. He is
my double.

дв-ою́родный, cousin

Мой двою́родный брат в
Пари́же. My cousin is in
Paris.

дв-ух'эта́жный, two-storeyed

Мы живём в двух'эта́жном
до́ме. We live in a two-
storeyed house.

ДВЕР-, ДВОР-, DOOR, COURT, YARD

двер-ь, door

Закро́йте дверь. Shut the
door.

пред-две́р-ие, beginning, entrance

Матема́тика — преддве́рие
астроно́мии. Mathematics
leads to (precedes) astron-
omy.

двор, courtyard, yard

Они́ игра́ли на дворе́. They
were playing in the yard.

двор-е́ц, palace

Царь постро́ил дворе́ц. **The tsar has built a palace.**

двор-е́цкий, butler

Дворе́цкий ждал нас у вхо́да. **The butler was awaiting us at the entrance.**

двор-ник, janitor

Дво́рник подмета́л ле́стницу. **The janitor was sweeping the stairway.**

двор-яни́н, nobleman, gentleman

Дворя́не игра́ли ви́дную роль в ста́рой Росси́и. **The nobility played an important role in old Russia.**

при-дво́р-ный, court

Он придво́рный врач. **He is a court physician.**

во-двор-я́ть, } to install, settle,
во-двор-и́ть, } bring about, establish

Годуно́в хоте́л водвори́ть поря́док в стране́. **Godunov wanted to establish order in the country.**

ДВИГ- MOVE

дви́г-ать, to move

Не дви́гайте рука́ми. **Don't move (your) hands.**

движ-е́ние, movement, traffic, motion

О́коло вокза́ла большо́е движе́ние. **There is much traffic near the station.**

дви́ж-имый, movable

Нало́г на дви́жимое иму́щество упла́чен. **The tax on the movable property has been paid.**

дви́-нуть (двиг-нуть), to move, push

Он дви́нул стул. **He moved (pushed) the chair.**

за-дви́ж-ка, latch, bolt, bar

Дверь за́перта на задви́жку. **The door is latched.**

по́-двиг, exploit, feat, deed

Вы соверши́ли геро́йский по́двиг. **You have done a heroic deed.**

на-двиг-а́ться, to draw near, approach

Надвига́ется гроза́. The thunderstorm is approaching.

ДЕ-. (ДѢ)-, DO, WORK, MAKE

де́-ло, business, affair, matter, concern

Како́е вам до э́того де́ло? What does it matter to you?

де́-лать, to do, make

Что он здесь де́лает? What is he doing here?

де-лово́й, business

У них делово́й разгово́р. They are having a business talk.

де́-льный, capable, clever

Он о́чень де́льный рабо́тник. He is a capable worker.

пере-де́-лка, repair, alteration

Необходи́мо отда́ть пла́тье в переде́лку. It is necessary to alter the dress.

де́-йствовать, to act, work, function

Так де́йствовать нельзя́. It is impossible to act this way.

де́-ятель, worker, public man, statesman

Его́ зять изве́стный полити́ческий де́ятель. His son-in-law is a prominent politician.

со-де́-йствие, assistance, help, cooperation

Окажи́те ему́ соде́йствие. Give him (your) assistance.

ДЕН-, DAY

ден-ь, day

Мы рабо́таем ка́ждый день. We work every day.

дн-ева́ть, to spend all one's time

Он дню́ет и ночу́ет там. He spends all his time there.

днев-ни́к, diary

Она́ ведёт дневни́к. She keeps a diary.

еже-дн-е́вный, daily

Мы получа́ем ежедне́вную газе́ту. We get a daily newspaper.

по-дён-ный, day, by the day, time-work

Она́ хо́дит на подённую рабо́ту. She works by the day.

по-полу́-дн-и, afternoon

Я приду́ к вам в три часа́ пополу́дни. I shall come to you at three o'clock in the afternoon.

ДЕРЕВ-, ДРЕВ-, ДРОВ-, WOOD, TREE

де́рев-о, tree

Како́е высо́кое де́рево. What a tall tree!

дерев-е́нский, village, country

Это дереве́нские ребя́та. These are the village children.

дере́в-ня, village

Они́ живу́т в дере́вне. They live in the village.

дерев-я́нный, wooden

Мы стро́им деревя́нный сара́й. We are building a wooden barn.

дре́в-о, tree

Дре́во позна́ния добра́ и зла. The tree of knowledge.

древ-е́сный, wood

Из древе́сной коры́ де́лают бума́гу. They make paper from the (wood) bark.

дров-а́, logs, firewood

Дрова́ горя́т я́рко. The logs burn brightly.

дро́в-ни, sled

Крестья́нин е́дет на дро́внях. The peasant is riding in a sled.

дре́в-ний, ancient

Они́ изуча́ют дре́внюю исто́рию. They are studying ancient history.

дре́в-ность, antiquity

В дре́вности не зна́ли желе́за. In (remote) antiquity they did not know iron.

из-древ-ле, in olden days, since time immemorial

Славя́не и́здревле отлича́лись гостеприи́мством. Since time immemorial the Slavs have been noted for their hospitality.

ДЕРЖ-, HOLD, RULE

держ-а́ва, power, state

А́нглия — вели́кая держа́ва. England is a great power.

держ-а́ть, to hold

Мать де́ржит ребёнка на рука́х. The mother holds the child in her arms.

вы́-держ-ать, to stand, pass

Моя́ сестра́ вы́держала экза́мен. My sister passed the examination.

за-держ-а́ть, to detain, stop

Поли́ция задержа́ла подозри́тельного челове́ка. The policemen have detained a suspicious person.

под-де́рж-ка, support, encouragement

Он рассчи́тывает на ва́шу подде́ржку. He counts on your support.

само-держ-а́вие, autocracy, absolutism

Революционе́ры вели́ борьбу́ про́тив самодержа́вия. The revolutionaries struggled against autocracy.

со-держ-а́ть, to support, keep, maintain

Она́ соде́ржит свои́х роди́телей. She supports her parents.

ДИВ-, WONDER

ди́в-о, marvel, wonder

Что за ди́во? What wonder?

ди́в-ный, wonderful, delightful

Пе́ред ни́ми откры́лся ди́вный вид. A wonderful view spread before them.

у-див-ля́ться, ⎫ to wonder, to   Я удивля́юсь ва́шему терпе́-
у-див-и́ться, ⎭   be amazed   нию. I am amazed at your
     patience.

у-див-ле́ние, amazement,   Он посмотре́л на неё с
astonishment, surprise   удивле́нием. He looked at
     her in amazement.

ДИК-, WILD

дик-а́рь, savage   Дикари́ встреча́ются и
     тепе́рь. One comes across
     savages even now.

ди́к-ий, wild   На о́зере мно́го ди́ких у́ток.
     There are many wild ducks
     on the lake.

ди́к-ость, savagery, brutality   Остро́вский описа́л ди́кость
     купе́ческих нра́вов. Os-
     trovsky described (pre-
     sented) the brutality of the
     life of the merchants.

ич-ь, game, nonsense   Они́ охо́тятся за ди́чью.
     They are hunting game.

     Что за дичь! What non-
     sense!

ДОЛГ-, DEBT

долг, debt   Я уже́ заплати́л долг. I
     have already paid (my)
     debt.

долж-ни́к, debtor   Тепе́рь он не должни́к. Now
     he is no longer a debtor.

до́лж-ность, position, employ-   Она́ получи́ла хоро́шую
ment   до́лжность. She has se-
     cured a good position.

за-долж-а́ться, to be in-   Мы о́чень задолжа́лись. We
debted, to run into debt   have run into debt.

о-долж-éние, favor, service

Пожáлуйста сдéлайте мне одолжéние. Please do me a favor.

ДОЛГ-, ДЛИН-, LONG

дóлг-ий, long

Дóлгое путешéствие нас утомúло. The long journey has fatigued us.

долг-отá, longitude

На какóй долготé нахóдится Ленингрáд? What is the longitude of Leningrad?

про-долж-áться, to continue, go on

Концéрт продолжáлся до полýночи. The concert went on until midnight.

длин-á, length

Он растянýлся во всю длинý. He sprawled his full length.

длúн-ный, long

В Сан Францúско óчень длúнный мост. The bridge in San Francisco is very long.

длú-тельный, lengthy, protracted, lingering

Длúтельный перúод болéзни. A lingering illness. A protracted period of illness.

ДОБ-, FIT

у-дóб-ный, convenient, favorable

Воспóльзуемся удóбным слýчаем. Let us take advantage of the favorable opportunity.

у-дóб-ство, convenience, comfort

У них квартúра со всéми удóбствами. They have an apartment with all the conveniences.

по-дóб-ный, similar, like

Я ничегó подóбного не вúдела. I have never seen anything like it.

с-до́б-ный, rich dough

К за́втраку по́дали сдо́бные бу́лки. For breakfast they served sweet buns.

ДОБР-, GOOD, KIND

до́бр-ый, good, kind

Его́ лю́бят за до́брый нрав. They like him for his kindness.

добр-оде́тель, virtue

Доброде́тель не всегда́ торжеству́ет. Virtue is not always triumphant.

добр-ота́, kindness, goodness

Я призна́телен за ва́шу доброту́. I am grateful for your kindness. I appreciate your kindness.

добр-о-со́вестный, conscientious

Она́ добросо́вестная студе́нтка. She is a conscientious student.

у-добр-е́ние, fertilizer

Эта по́чва нужда́ется в удобре́нии. This soil needs fertilizing.

ДОМ-, HOME, HOUSE

дом, home, house

У нас со́бственный дом. We have our own home.

дом-а́шний, domestic, homemade

Ко́шка — дома́шнее живо́тное. The cat is a domestic animal.

дом-ово́й, house spirit

В домовы́х и тепе́рь ещё ве́рят. Even now some believe in house spirits.

дом-осе́д, stay-at-home

Мой муж домосе́д. My husband is a stay-at-home person.

ДР-, ДАР-, ДИР-, ДОР-, ДЫР-, TEAR, BREAK

др-а́ка, fight

На ми́тинге произошла́ дра́ка. There was a fight at the meeting.

др-а́ться, to fight

Де́ти деру́тся на у́лице. Children are fighting on the street.

др-ачу́н, fighter, bully, squabbler

Ва́нька большо́й драчу́н. Vanya is a great bully.

у-да́р, blow

Он нанёс ей си́льный уда́р. He dealt her a severe blow.

у-дар-е́ние, accent, stress

Ударе́ние(лежи́т) на второ́м сло́ге. The accent falls on the second syllable.

у-дар-я́ть, ⎱ to beat, strike,
у-да́р-ить, ⎰   ring, toll

Уда́рили в ко́локол. They tolled the bell. (The bells tolled.)

при-ди́р-ка,   fault-finding, cavil, quibble

Э́то не бо́льше как приди́рка. This is merely a quibble.

раз-дир-а́ть, to tear, break

Её слёзы раздира́ют мне се́рдце. Her tears break my heart.

вз-дор, nonsense

По́лно говори́ть вам вздор. Stop talking nonsense.

за-до́р, fervour, heat, energy

Он рабо́тал с ю́ношеским задо́ром. He worked with youthful fervour.

раз-до́р, discord, quarrel

Ме́жду ни́ми раздо́р.   A discord rose between them

дыр-а́, hole

Я заштопала дыру́. I have darned the hole.

дыр-я́вый, torn, ragged

На ней бы́ло дыря́вое пла́тье. She wore a ragged dress.

обо-др-а́нец, tramp

Ко мне подошёл ободра́нец. A tramp came up to me.

ДРАЗ-, TEASE

драз-нить, to tease

Не дразните собаку. Don't tease the dog.

раз-драж-а́ть, to irritate

Шум раздража́ет меня́. The noise irritates me.

раз-драж-е́ние, exasperation, irritation

В поры́ве раздраже́ния он наговори́л де́рзостей. In a moment of exasperation he made impertinent re marks.

ДРОГ-, SHUDDER, TREMBLE

дро́г-нуть, to shudder, tremble, hesitate

У него́ не дро́гнет рука́ уби́ть её. His hand will not hesitate to kill her. (He will make no scruple to kill her.)

дрож-а́ть, to tremble, shake, shiver

Переста́ньте дрожа́ть. Stop shivering.

дрож-ь, trembling, shiver, shudder

Меня́ охвати́ла дрожь. I shiver.

вз-дра́г-ивать, } to start,
вз-дро́г-нуть, } wince

Она́ вздро́гнула от испу́га. She started in fear.

про-дро́г-нуть, to be chilled, to be chilled to the marrow

Мы промо́кли и продро́гли. We got wet and were chilled to the marrow.

ДРУГ-, ДОРОГ-, FRIEND, DEAR, ROAD

друг, friend

Ста́рый друг лу́чше но́вых двух. An old friend is better than two new ones.

дру́ж-ба, friendship

Ме́жду ни́ми завяза́лась те́сная дру́жба. An intimate friendship sprang up between them.

друж-еский, friendly

Вот вам дру́жеский сове́т. Here is my friendly advice to you.

дружж-и́на, bodyguard

Князь пиру́ет с дружи́ной. The prince feasts with his bodyguard.

друж-и́ть, to be friends with, to be on friendly terms

Я бо́льше не дружу́ с ней. I am no longer her friend.

дорог-о́й, dear

Дорого́й мой друг. My dear friend.

дорож-а́ть, to rise in price

Тепе́рь всё дорожа́ет. Now everything is rising in price.

дорож-и́ть, to value, prize

Я дорожу́ ва́шим внима́нием. I value (appreciate) your attention (favor).

драг-о-це́нный, precious

Кольцо́ с драгоце́нным ка́мнем. The ring with a precious stone.

доро́г-а, road

Мы е́здили по большо́й доро́ге. We were driving along the highway.

доро́ж-ный, travelling

Захвати́те ваш доро́жный костю́м. Take your travelling suit.

ДУ-, ДУХ-, ДЫХ-, BLOW, BREATH, SPIRIT

ду-нове́ние, whiff, breath

Дунове́ние ветерка́ разбуди́ло меня́. A whiff of wind awoke me.

ду-ть, to blow

Здесь ду́ет. There is a draught here.

на-ду-ва́ть,
на-ду́-ть, } to deceive, fool

Адвока́т наду́л своего́ клие́нта. The lawyer deceived his customer.

о-ду-ва́нчик, dandelion

Одува́нчик растёт в по́ле. A dandelion grows in the field.

дух, spirit, mind

Он сохранйл бόдрость дýха. He has preserved his mental vigour.

дух-όвный, spiritual

Нельзя жить однόй духόвной пйщей. One cannot live on spiritual food alone.

душ-á, soul

Говорйли о бессмéртии душй. They spoke about the immortality of the soul.

душ-йть, to choke, suffocate

Меня дýшат слёзы. Tears choke me.

дых-áние, breathing

У неё захватйло дыхáние. She was out of breath.

όт-дых, rest

Им необходйм όтдых. They must have a rest.

от-дых-áть, }
от-дох-нýть, } to rest

Порабόтали, порá и отдохнýть. You have done the work, now it's time to rest.

о-душ-евлять, } to animate,
о-душ-евйть, } inspire

Поэты чáсто одушевляют прирόду. Poets often animate nature.

ДУМ-, THOUGHT

дýм-а, thought, meditation

Дόлгая дýма, лйшняя скорбь. A long meditation brings unnecessary sadness.

дýм-ать, to think, ponder

О чём вы дýмаете? What are you thinking about?

вы́-дум-ать, to invent, devise

Я не вы́думал этого. I did not invent it.

за-дýм-чивость, thoughtfulness, musing

Онá ходйла в задýмчивости. She walked about musing.

об-дýм-ать, to think, consider

Этот вопрόс нáдо обдýмать. We must consider this matter.

при-ду́м-ать, to devise, concoct, invent

Приду́мали-ли вы что́-нибудь? Have you concocted anything?

ДУР-, FOOL

ду́р-а, foolish woman

Что за ду́ра! What a fool! (What a foolish woman!)

дур-а́к, fool

Он уж не тако́й дура́к. He is not such a fool.

дур-но́й, bad, poor

Не подава́йте дурно́го приме́ра. Don't give a bad example.

дур-и́ть, to fool

Вы всё дури́те. You are still fooling.

дур-ь, rubbish, foolishness

Его́ голова́ наби́та ду́рью. His head is stuffed with foolishness.

о-дур-е́ть, to grow stupid

От ста́рости он совсе́м одуре́л. Because of age he has grown quite stupid.

с-ду́р-у, out of stupidity

Она́ сболтну́ла сду́ру. She blabbed out of stupidity.

Е

ЕД-, (ѢД)-, ЯД-, FOOD, POISON

ед-а́, food

Еда́ ему́ не впрок. The food does not do him any good.

е́д-кий, biting, sharp, caustic

Он изве́стен свое́й е́дкой иро́нией. He is known for his caustic irony.

е-сть, to eat

Она́ совсе́м переста́ла есть. She has stopped eating. (She has completely lost her appetite.)

с'е-до́б-ный, (съѣд-доб-ный), edible

Эти грибы́ с'едо́бны. These mushrooms are edible.

об-е́д, dinner

Обе́д на столе́. The dinner is on the table.

об-е́д-ня, mass

В це́ркви слу́жат обе́дню. They are saying mass in the church.

надо-ед-а́ть,⎫to weary, tire,
надо-е́-сть, ⎭ annoy

Эта рабо́та мне надое́ла. This work wearies me.

надо-е́д-ливый, tiresome, annoying

Како́й вы надое́дливый челове́к. What a tiresome person you are.

яд, poison

Вме́сто лека́рства ей да́ли яд. Instead of medicine they gave her poison.

яд-ови́тый, poisonous, venomous

Ядови́тая змея́ ползла́ по траве́. A venomous snake was crawling in the grass.

я́-ства, food, viands

На блю́дах по́дали вку́сные я́ства. Tasty viands were served on platters.

ЕДИН-, ОДИН-, ONE, UNIT

един-е́ние, unity

В едине́нии си́ла. In unity there is power.

един-и́ца, unit

До́ллар — де́нежная едини́ца. The dollar is a monetary unit.

един-и́чный, unique

Это едини́чный слу́чай. This case is unique.

еди́н-ство, unity, union, concord, unanimity

Вам изве́стно еди́нство на́ших стремле́ний. You know the unanimity of our aspirations.

об'един-и́ть, to unite, unify

Опа́сность их об'едини́ла. Danger united them.

у-един-éние, solitude, retirement

Он жил в уединéнии. He lived in solitude. (He lived a solitary life.)

одúн, one, single

Одúн в пóле не вóин. One soldier does not make a regiment.

один-óкий, one, alone, solitary, lonely

В оврáге стоúт одинóкий дóмик. There is a lonely little house in the ravine.

один-óчество, solitude, single life, loneliness

Я обречён на одинóчество. I am doomed to loneliness.

одн-áжды, once

Однáжды онá чуть не утонýла. Once she was almost drowned.

ЕЗД-, (ѢЗД)-, RIDE

езд-á, ride, riding, driving

Меня утомляет верховáя езда. Horseback riding tires me.

éзд-ить, to ride, drive

Мы éздим в гóрод кáждый день. We drive (go) to the city every day.

езд-óк, rider, horseman

Вы прекрáсный ездóк. You are an excellent horseman.

é-хать, to ride, travel

Онú éхали по желéзной дорóге. They went (travelled) by train.

вы-езж-áть, ⎰ to go away,
вы́-е-хать, ⎱ leave, move out

Мы выезжáем из э́той квартúры. We are moving out of this apartment.

на-éзд-ница, equestrienne

Цирковáя наéздница упáла с лóшади. The circus equestrienne fell down (off her horse).

под'-éзд, porch, entrance

Швейцáр стоя́л у под'éзда. The porter stood at the entrance.

при-е́зд, arrival, coming

Мы ждём прие́зда отца́. We are expecting (the arrival of) our father.

про-е́зд, passage, fare

Я заплачу́ за ваш прое́зд. I am going to pay for your passage.

у-е́зд, district

В на́шем уе́зде мно́го иностра́нцев. There are many foreigners in our district.

ЕМ-, ИМ-, Я-, POSSESS, HAVE

за-ём, loan

В ба́нке мо́жно сде́лать заём. One can get a loan at the bank.

за-и́м-ствовать, to imitate, borrow

Он мно́го заи́мствовал от Го́голя. He borrowed a great deal from Gogol.

за-н-им-а́ть, }
за-н-я́-ть, } to borrow

Займи́те для меня́ э́ти де́ньги. Borrow this money for me.

им-е́ть, to have

Он име́ет о вас дурно́е мне́ние. He has a poor opinion of you.

им-е́ние, estate

Их име́ние про́дано с торга́. Their estate was auctioned off.

им-у́щество, property, belongings

Всё её иму́щество сгоре́ло. She lost all her belongings in the fire.

вн-им-а́ние, attention

Обрати́те внима́ние на э́то. Pay attention to this.

вос-при-н-им-а́ть, to take, perceive, to be receptive, to be susceptible

Ребёнок бы́стро воспринима́ет впечатле́ния. A child is very susceptible to impressions. A child quickly receives impressions.

на-ём, rent, hiring, lease

Э́та ко́мната отдаётся в наём. This room is for rent.

на-н-им-а́ть, ⎫
⎬ to hire
на-н-я́-ть, ⎭

В конто́ре нанима́ют слу́жащих. In the office they are hiring employees.

Нам на́до наня́ть прислу́гу We must hire a maid.

под'-ём, ascent, rise

На́ гору был круто́й под'ём. The ascent up the hill was steep.

под-н-им-а́ть, ⎫
⎬ to lift, raise, heave
под-н-я́-ть, ⎭

Я поднима́ю тя́жесть. I am lifting a heavy load.

Ему́ бы́ло хо́лодно и он по́днял воротни́к. He was cold, and he turned up (raised) his collar.

при-ём, reception, office-hours, hours of business

У до́ктора приём от девяти́ часо́в утра́. The physician's office hours start at nine in the morning.

при-н-им-а́ть, ⎫
⎬ to receive, entertain
при-н-я́-ть, ⎭

Они́ ча́сто принима́ют госте́й. They often entertain visitors.

Его́ при́няли раду́шно. He received a hearty welcome.

при-я́-тель, friend

Э́то мой прия́тель. This is my friend.

при-я́-тный, pleasant

Мы получи́ли прия́тную но́вость. We received pleasant news.

сн-им-а́ть, ⎫
⎬ to take, take off
сн-я́-ть, ⎭

Я снима́ю пальто́. I am taking off my coat.

С него́ сня́ли фотогра́фию. They took his picture (his photograph).

сн-и́м-ок, photograph, snap-shot

Э́тот сни́мок неуда́чен. This is a bad (poor) photograph.

Ж

ЖАД-, GREED

жа́д-ничать, to be greedy

Не́чего вам жа́дничать. You don't have to be greedy.

жа́д-ность, greed, avidity, cupidity

Он ел с жа́дностью. He ate greedily (with greed).

жа́д-ный, greedy, rapacious

Вся́кий зна́ет что во́лки жа́дны. Everybody knows that wolves are greedy.

жа́жд-а, thirst, craving

Меня́ томи́ла жа́жда. I suffered from thirst.

жа́жд-ать, to thirst, crave, long for

Он жа́ждет сла́вы. He is longing for fame.

ЖАЛ-, PITY, FAVOR, PLAINT

жал-е́ть, to pity, to be sorry, regret

Она́ жале́ет э́ту сироту́. She pities this orphan.

жа́л-кий, pitiful, sad, sorry, lamentable

Семья́ нахо́дится в жа́лком положе́нии. The family is in a sorry plight.

жа́л-оба, complaint, grievance

Мы по́дали на него́ жа́лобу. We made a complaint about him.

жа́л-обный, plaintive, sad

Послы́шался жа́лобный крик A plaintive cry was heard.

жал-ь, what a pity, pity, (I am) sorry

О́чень жаль, что вы не пришли́. What a pity that you did not come!

со-жал-е́ние, pity, compassion, regret

Она́ посмотре́ла на них с сожале́нием. She looked at them with compassion.

со-жал-е́ть, to regret, to be sorry

Я сожале́ю что так вы́шло. I am sorry that it happened so.

жа́л-о, sting

Нет пчелы́ без жа́ла. There is no bee without a sting.

жа́л-ование,
жа́л-ованье, } pay, salary

Ему́ приба́вили жа́лованье. They gave him a raise.

жа́л-овать, to give, grant, favor, like

Про́сим его́ люби́ть и жа́ловать. We beg you to be kind and gracious to him.

ЖАР-, HEAT

жар- heat, temperature, fever, ardor

У меня́ си́льный жар. I have a high temperature. (I am running a fever.)

жар-а́, heat

Стоя́ла невыноси́мая жара́. It was unbearably hot.

жа́р-ить, to fry

Куха́рка жа́рит ры́бу. The cook is frying the fish.

жа́р-кий, hot, warm

Сего́дня жа́ркий день. Today is a warm day. (It is hot today.)

по-жа́р, fire

Вчера́ был большо́й пожа́р. There was a big fire yesterday.

по-жа́р-ный, fireman

Пожа́рный упа́л с ле́стницы. The fireman fell from the ladder.

ЖГ-, ЖЕГ-, ЖИГ-, ЖОГ-, BURN

жг-у́чий, burning, scorching, smarting

Жгу́чая боль не даёт мне поко́я. The smarting pain gives me no rest.

жеч-ь (жег-ть), to burn

Мы жжём дрова́. We are burning the logs.

с-жиг-а́ть,
с-жеч-ь, } to burn

Они́ сожгли́ все докуме́нты. They burned all the documents.

раз-жиг-а́ть, to kindle, inflame, start

Го́рничная разжига́ет камин. The maid is starting the fire in the fireplace.

со-жж-е́ние (со-жьг-ение), burning, cremation

В Индии тру́пы предаю́тся сожже́нию. In India the dead are cremated.

со-жж-ённый, scorched, burnt

Сожжённая со́лнцем трава́ побле́кла. The grass scorched in the sun has wilted.

из-жо́г-а, heartburn

Всю ночь его́ му́чила изжо́га. All night long he suffered from heartburn.

под-жо́г, arson, setting fire

Их суди́ли за подж́ог. They were tried for arson.

ЖЕЛ-, WISH

жел-а́ние, wish, desire, accord, will

Я поступи́л так по моему́ со́бственному жела́нию. I acted thus in accordance with my own wishes (will) (at my will).

жел-а́-тельный, desirable

Ва́ше прису́тствие бы́ло бы о́чень жела́тельно. Your presence would be very desirable.

жел-а́ть, to wish

Жела́ю вам сча́стья. I wish you happiness. (I wish you good luck.)

благо-жел-а́тель, well-wisher, well-disposed

Смирно́в его́ благожела́тель. Smirnov is his well-wisher.

добро-жел-а́тельный, benevolent, friendly, well-wishing

Спаси́бо вам за ва́ше добро-жела́тельное отноше́ние. Thank you for your friendly attitude (for your kindness).

по-жел-а́ние, wish

Мы шлём вам наилу́чшие пожела́ния. We are sending you our best wishes.

по-жел-а́ть, to wish

Позво́льте пожела́ть вам
счастли́вого пути́.   May
I wish you a happy journey.

ЖЕЛТ-, YELLOW

желт-е́ть, to yellow

Вдали́ желте́ет подсо́лнух. A
sunflower yellows in the
distance.

желт-о́к, yolk

Возьми́те два желтка́. Take
two yolks.

желт-у́ха, jaundice

Мой сын бо́лен желту́хой.
My son suffers from jaundice.

жёлт-ый, yellow

На ней жёлтое пла́тье. She
is wearing a yellow dress.

жёлч-ь, gall, bile

У него́ разлила́сь жёлчь.
He has trouble with his
gall bladder.

жёлч-ный, bilious, irritable,
choleric, irascible

Како́й вы жёлчный челове́к.
How irritable you are.

по-желт-е́ть, to grow yellow,
become yellow

Трава́ пожелте́ла. The grass
has turned yellow.

ЖЕЛЕЗ-, (ЖЕЛѢЗ)-, IRON

желе́з-о, iron

В э́тих гора́х добыва́ют
желе́зо. In these mountains
iron (ore) is mined.

желе́з-ный, iron

Росси́я бога́та железно́й
рудо́й. Russia abounds in
iron ore.

желез-ня́к, bloodstone, hematite

Железня́к краснова́того цве́-
та. The hematite is of a
reddish color.

желез-но-доро́жный, railway,
railroad

В э́той дере́вне нет железно-
доро́жной ста́нции. There
is no railway station in
this village.

ЖЕН-, WOMAN

жен-а́, wife

У него́ молода́я жена́. He has a young wife.

жен-а́тый, married

Жена́тый челове́к забо́тится о свое́й семье́. A married man takes care of his family.

жен-и́ть, to marry

Вот мы его́ и жени́ли. And so we married him.

жен-и́-тьба, marriage

Они́ заговори́ли о жени́тьбе. They began to talk about marriage.

жен-и́х, bridegroom

В це́ркви ждут жениха́. The bridegroom is expected at the church.

же́н-ский, feminine, woman's

Э́то де́ло же́нское. This is a woman's occupation. (This is a woman's concern.)

же́н-ственность, effeminacy

Его́ же́нственность по́ртит ему́ карье́ру. His effeminacy is ruining his career.

же́н-щина, woman

Она́ хоро́шая же́нщина. She is a nice woman.

ЖЕРТ-, ЖР-, SACRIFICE

же́рт-ва, victim, sacrifice

Мне же́ртвы не нужны́. I do not want (need) sacrifice.

же́рт-вовать, to sacrifice

Он же́ртвует свое́й жи́знью. He sacrifices his life.

по-же́рт-вование, offering, donation, gift

Здесь собира́ют поже́ртвования. Donations are accepted here.

жр-ец, priest, druid

Жрец заколо́л ягнёнка. The priest slaughtered the lamb.

жр-е́ческий, priest's, priestly

Жре́ческий жезл лежа́л о́коло алтаря́. The priest's staff lay near the altar.

ЖЕСТ-, STIFF, HARD

жёст-кий, stiff, hard, tough

Щётка из жёсткой щети́ны. The brush (made) of stiff bristles.

жест-о́кий, cruel, harsh

Жесто́кий никого́ не жале́ет. A cruel person does not pity anyone.

жест-ь, tin

Э́та кру́жка сде́лана из же́сти. This jug is made of tin.

жест-я́нка, tin, tin can

За неиме́нием стака́на мы пи́ли из жестя́нки. For lack of a glass we drank out of a tin can.

жест-яно́й, tin, pewter

На столе́ была́ жестяна́я посу́да. There were some tin dishes on the table.

ЖИ-, LIFE

жи-знь, life, living, existence

Жизнь его́ висе́ла на волоске́. His life was hanging by a thread.

жи́-тель, inhabitant, resident, dweller

Жи́тели городо́в всегда́ спеша́т. The city dwellers are always in a hurry.

жи-ть, to live, stay, exist

Мы живём недалеко́ отсю́да. We live not far from here.

жи-тьё, life, existence

Их житьё не сла́дкое. Their life is not easy.

жи-во́й, living

В дере́вне мы не встре́тили ни одно́й живо́й души́. In the village we did not meet a single person (a single living soul).

жи-во́т, stomach, abdomen

У ребёнка боли́т живо́т. The child has a stomachache.

жи-во́т-ное, animal

Я люблю́ живо́тных. I like animals.

жи-ву́чий, tenacious of life

Он живу́ч, как ко́шка. He has nine lives like a cat.

жи-ле́ц, tenant, boarder

Наш жиле́ц инжене́р. Our tenant is an engineer.

жи-ли́ще, abode, dwelling, residence

Не ви́дно ни одного́ жили́ща. Not a single dwelling was to be seen.

вы́-жи-ть, to survive, drive out, get rid, turn out

Мы наси́лу его́ вы́жили. We could hardly get rid of him.

жи́-вопись, painting

Я интересу́юсь жи́вописью. I am interested in painting.

на́-жи-ва, gain, profit

Э́тот деле́ц го́нится то́лько за на́живой. This businessman is looking only for profit.

по-жи-ло́й, middle-aged

Учи́тель, пожило́й челове́к, вы́шел в отста́вку. The teacher, a middle-aged man, resigned.

у-жи́-ться, to live in harmony, to live peacefully, to get on

С таки́ми людьми́ тру́дно ужи́ться. With such people it is difficult to live peacefully. (It is difficult to get on with such people.)

3

ЗВ-, ЗОВ-, ЗЫВ-, CALL

зв-а́ние, calling, social position, rank

Сюда́ собра́лись лю́ди вся́кого зва́ния. People of all walks of life gathered here.

зв-ать, to call, name

Как вас звать? (Как вас зову́т?) What is your name?

воз-зв-áние, proclamation

Мы читáли воззвáние. We were reading the proclamation.

на-зв-áть, to name

Он непрáвильно назвáл э́тот минерáл. He named this mineral incorrectly.

по-зв-áть, to call, summon

Я позовý вас когдá вы мне бýдете нужны́. I shall call you when I need you.

со-зв-áть, to summon, invite, call

Нáдо созвáть комитéт. We must call the committee. (It is necessary to call the committee.)

зов, call, summons, invitation

Вы не отвéтили на мой зов. You did not answer my call.

вы́-зов, challenge, defiance, summons

В егó словáх слы́шался вы́зов. Defiance was heard in his words.

вы-зыв-áть, to call, call up, send for, evoke

Меня́ вызывáют по телефóну. Someone is calling me over the telephone. (I am wanted on the 'phone.)

óт-зыв, reference, mention, declaration, recall, recommendation, record

О вас имéются лéстные óтзывы. We have a good record about you.

ЗВОН-, ЗВ-, ЗВУК-, RINGING, SOUND

звон, ringing, sound

Я услы́шал звон разби́той посýды. I heard the sound of broken dishes.

звон-и́ть, to peal, toll, ring

Звоня́т в колоколá. They are ringing the bells.

звен-éть, to ring, clank, tinkle

Пóрваная струнá звени́т. The broken string is ringing.

звóн-кий, loud, clear

Орáтор говори́л звóнким гóлосом. The orator spoke in a clear voice.

звон-о́к, bell

Послы́шался звоно́к в дверя́х. The bell rang at the door.

звон-а́рь, bell-ringer

Звона́рь подня́лся на колоко́льню. The bell-ringer climbed to the belfry.

по-звон-и́ть, to ring up, call up

Позвони́те ему́ по телефо́ну. Call him up over the 'phone.

до-звон-и́ться, to ring up

Я ника́к не могу́ дозвони́ться. I cannot get any answer.

звук, sound, tone

И́з лесу доно́сятся таи́нственные зву́ки. Mysterious sounds come from the woods.

звук-ово́й, sound, sounding

Звуковы́е во́лны передаю́тся по ра́дио. The sound waves are transmitted over the radio.

звуч-а́ть, to sound

Э́тот роя́ль звучи́т осо́бенно хорошо́. This piano sounds particularly well. (The tone of this piano is particularly good.)

звуч-ный, loud, resonant, deep-toned

Э́то зву́чный инструме́нт. This instrument has a good tone.

звуч-ность, sonorousness

По зву́чности италья́нский язы́к стои́т на пе́рвом ме́сте. For its sonorousness the Italian language ranks first.

ЗВЕР-, BEAST

звер-и́нец, menagerie, zoological garden

В воскресе́нье мы бы́ли в звери́нце. On Sunday we were at the zoological garden.

звер-и́ный, animal, wild

В Сиби́ри занима́ются зве-ри́ным про́мыслом.   In Siberia they hunt wild animals.

звер-ь, animal

Они́ охо́тились на пушны́х звере́й. They were hunting the fur-bearing animals.

звер-ство, brutality

Кто спосо́бен на тако́е звер-ство? Who is capable of such brutality?

звер-ствовать, to behave with brutality, to be cruel, bru-tal

Что он так звер́ствует? Why is he so brutal?

ЗД-, BUILD, CREATE

зд-а́ние, building

Архите́ктор вы́строил но́вое зда́ние.   The architect has constructed a new building.

со-зд-а́ние, creature

Како́е ми́лое созда́ние! What a dear little creature!

со-зд-а́тель, creator, author

Маркс созда́тель но́вого эко-номи́ческого уче́ния. Marx is the author of the new economic theory.

ЗДОРОВ-, ЗДРАВ- HEALTH

здоро́в-ый, healthy, sound

Здоро́вому ничего́ не с ра́ш-но.   A healthy man is not afraid of anything.

здоро́в-ье, health

Как ва́ше здоро́вье?   How are you?   (How is your health?)

вы́-здоров-еть, to get well, recover

Она́ ско́ро вы́здоровела. She got well soon.

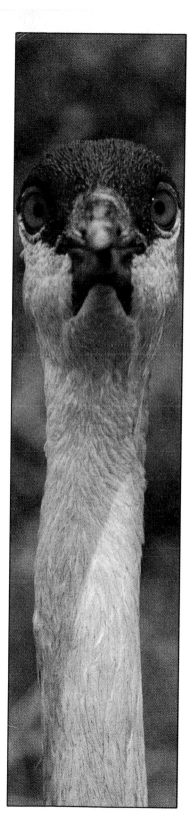

hake Я заме́тил его́ когда́ он здоро́вался с гостя́ми. I noticed him when he was greeting (shaking hands with) the guests.

well, Здра́вствуйте! How do you do? (How are you?)

Дай Бог вам здра́вствовать надо́лго. May the Lord grant you a long life.

У него́ здра́вый рассу́док. He has a sound mind.

ulate Позво́льте поздра́вить вас. Let me congratulate you.

I(EH)-, GREEN

Она́ напои́ла меня́ каки́м-то зе́льем. She gave me some kind of a potion to drink.

reen, Всё зелене́ет вокру́г. Everything round us looks green.

Морска́я вода́ ка́жется зеленова́тою. The salt (sea) water seems to be greenish.

На дере́вьях уже́ видна́ зелёная листва́. Green foliage has already appeared on the trees.

Зеленщи́к продаёт о́вощи. The greengrocer sells vegetables.

Вам ну́жно есть побо́льше зе́лени. You must eat more (green) vegetables.

ЗЕМ-, EARTH

зем-ля́, earth, soil, ground — Снег ещё лежи́т на земле́. The snow is still on the ground.

зем-ля́к, fellow countryman — Серге́й мой земля́к. Sergey is my countryman.

зем-ляни́ка, strawberry — Земляни́ка вку́сная я́года. The strawberry is tasty.

зем-ля́нка, mud hut — Они́ жи́ли в земля́нке. They lived in a mud hut.

зем-но́й, earthly, terrestrial — Земно́й шар враща́ется вокру́г оси́. The earth turns around its axis.

зем-ле-владе́лец, landowner — Землевладе́лец осма́тривает свой поля́. The landowner inspects (surveys) his fields.

зем-ле-де́лие, tilling, agriculture — Крестья́не занима́ются земледе́лием. The peasants are cultivating the land.

зем-ле-трясе́ние, earthquake — В Калифо́рнии ча́сто быва́ют землетрясе́ния. There are frequent earthquakes in California.

под-зе́м-ный, underground, subterranean — Тут идёт подзе́мная желе́зная доро́га. The subway runs here.

ту-зе́м-ец, native, aborigines — В Сиби́ри мно́го тузе́мцев. There are many aborigines in Siberia.

ЗИ-, ЗЕ-, GAPE, OPEN, YAWN

зи-я́ть, to gape, yawn, open — Пе́ред ни́ми зия́ла про́пасть. A precipice yawned before them.

зи-я́ющий, gaping, open — Я уви́дел зия́ющую ра́ну. I saw an open wound.

зев-а́ка, lounger, idler

По у́лице ходи́ла толпа́ зева́к. A throng of idlers moved along the street.

зев-а́ть,
зе́в-ну́ть, } to yawn

Я всё вре́мя зева́ю. I am yawning all the time.

Он раз зевну́л и засну́л. He yawned once and fell asleep.

зев-ота́, yawn

Она́ подави́ла зевоту́. She stifled a yawn.

про-зев-а́ть, to miss

Мы прозева́ли наш по́езд. We missed our train.

рото-зе́й, loafer

Ротозе́й попа́л в кана́ву. The loafer fell into a ditch.

ЗЛ-, EVIL, WICKED, ANGRY

зл-ить, to anger, provoke, vex, irritate

Не зли меня́. Don't vex me.

зл-о, evil, harm, ill, wrong

Я не жела́ю ему́ зла. I do not wish him harm.

зл-о́ба, fury, malice, spite, wickedness

В его́ груди́ кипе́ла зло́ба. He was boiling over with spite.

зл-о́бный, wicked, malicious, angry

Вы бро́сили на неё зло́бный взгляд. You looked angrily (daggers) at her.

зл-ой, evil, wicked

У неё злой нрав. She has a wicked temper.

зл-ость, anger, ill-naturedness

Я да́же покрасне́л от зло́сти. I even turned red with anger.

зл-ю́ка, spitfire

Ну и злю́ка же ты! What a spitfire you are!

зл-ю́щий, furious

Он верну́лся домо́й злю́щий презлю́щий. He came home simply furious.

зл-о-де́й, rascal, villain, malevolent person

Кто сам себе́ злоде́й? Who wishes harm to himself?

зл-о-па́мятный, spiteful, rancorous

Злопа́мятный челове́к и́щет ме́сти. A spiteful man looks for revenge.

зл-о-умы́шленник, malefactor

Злоумы́шленника уличи́ли. The malefactor was caught red-handed.

о-зл-о-бле́ние, anger, wrath, exasperation

Озлобле́ние наро́да привело́ к револю́ции. The people's wrath led to a revolution.

ЗНА-, KNOW

зна-к, sign, token, mark, symbol

В знак согла́сия он кивну́л голово́й. He nodded his head as a sign of consent.

зна-ко́мый, acquaintance

Э́тот господи́н мой знако́мый. This gentleman is an acquaintance of mine.

зна-мени́тый, famous, distinguished

Он знамени́тый хиру́рг. He is a famous surgeon.

зна́-мя, banner

Рабо́чие несли́ кра́сное зна́мя. The workmen were carrying a red banner.

зна́-ние, knowledge, learning, science

Вся́кое де́ло тре́бует зна́ния. Any kind of work requires knowledge (skill).

зна-ть, to know, to be informed, to be skilled

Нельзя́ всего́ знать. One cannot know everything.

зна́-чить, to mean

Что э́то зна́чит? What does it mean?

на-зна-ча́ть, to appoint

Его́ назнача́ют нача́льником отде́ла. He was appointed the head of the department.

по-зна-ко́мить, to acquaint, make one's acquaintance, to introduce

Я хочу́ вас познако́мить с ни́ми. I want to introduce you to them.

при́-зна-к, sign, token

Она́ не подава́ла при́знаков жи́зни. She gave no signs of life.

раз-у-зна́-ть, to learn, find out

Я постара́юсь разузна́ть об э́том. I shall try to find out about this.

со-зна́-ва́ть, to be conscious of, acknowledge, feel

Они́ сознаю́т свои́ оши́бки. They are conscious of their faults (mistakes).

ЗР-, ЗАР-, ЗЕР-, ЗИР-, ЗОР-, SEE, LOOK, LIGHT

зар-ни́ца, heat lightning

Вот вспы́хнула зарни́ца. The heat lightning flashed.

зар-я́, sunset, sunrise

Вече́рняя заря́ окра́сила не́бо. The sunset colored the sky.

о-зар-я́ть, о-зар-и́ть, { to illumine, brighten, light up

Лу́нный свет озаря́ет ко́мнату. Moonlight illumines the room.

зе́р-кало, mirror

Она́ смотре́лась в зе́ркало. She was looking into the mirror.

со-зер-ца́тельный, contemplative

У него́ созерца́тельная нату́ра. His is a contemplative nature.

в-зир-а́ть, to look at, regard

Он пошёл туда́ не взира́я на моё предостереже́ние. He went there in spite of (disregarding) my warning.

над-зир-а́тель, inspector, superintendent, warden

Надзира́тель проха́живался по коридо́ру. The superintendent was walking along the corridor.

пре-зир-а́ть, to despise, scorn	Не презира́йте меня́. Don't despise me.
в-зор, look, glance, gaze	Она́ поту́пила свой взор She cast her eyes down.
до-зо́р, patrol, round	Солда́ты хо́дят дозо́ром. The sentries are making their rounds.
по-зо́р, disgrace	Э́то позо́р для нас всех. This is a disgrace for all of us.
у-зо́р pattern, design	Я вышива́ю узо́р. I am embroidering a pattern.
зр-е́лище, spectacle, show, sight	Како́е чу́дное зре́лище! What a wonderful sight!
зр-е́ние, sight, vision, eye-sight	У него́ плохо́е зре́ние. His eyesight is poor (bad).
обо-зр-е́ние, review, survey	В газе́те вы найдёте обо-зре́ние ва́жных собы́тий. In the newspaper you will find a survey of important events.
подо-зр-е́ние, distrust, sus-picion	Э́тот господи́н нахо́дится под подозре́нием. This man is under suspicion. (This man is suspected.)
пре-зр-е́ние, scorn, contempt	Вы отно́ситесь к ним с презре́нием. You are treating them with scorn. (You scorn them.)
при́-зр-ак, ghost, phantom	Его́ трево́жат при́зраки про́шлого. The phantoms of the past are troubling him.
при́-зр-ачный, illusory, un-real	Она́ прельща́ет себя́ при́-зрачными наде́ждами. She is deceiving herself with illusory hopes.

при-зр-е́ние, protection, charity	В на́шем го́роде два до́ма для призре́ния бе́дных. In our town there are two charitable institutions for the poor.

И

ИГР-, GAME, PLAY

игр-а́, game, play	Я предпочита́ю игру́ на скри́пке. I prefer playing the violin.
игр-а́ть, to play	Де́ти игра́ют в мяч. The children are playing ball.
игр-и́-вый, playful	Игри́вые во́лны набега́ют на́ бе́рег. The playful waves beat against the shore.
игр-о́к, gambler, player	Он аза́ртный игро́к. He is a gambler.
игр-у́шка, plaything, toy	У неё нет игру́шек. She has no toys.
вы-и́гр-ыш, winnings, gain, prize	Э́то мой вы́игрыш. This is my prize. (These are my winnings.)
про-игр-а́ть, to lose, to play	Он проигра́л всё своё состоя́ние. He lost (at cards) his entire fortune.
с-ыгр-а́ть (съ-игр-ать), to play	Что вам сыгра́ть? What shall I play (for you)?

ИН-, OTHER, DIFFERENT

ин-а́че, or else, otherwise	Беги́те, ина́че вы опозда́ете. Run (Hurry), otherwise (or else) you will be late.
ин-огда́, sometimes, occasionally	Иногда́ они́ купа́ются в мо́ре. Occasionally they bathe in the sea.

ин-о́й, different, other

А, э́то ино́й разгово́р. Ah, this is quite a different talk.

ИСК-, ЫСК-, SEEK

иск, suit, action, claim

Ему́ пред'яви́ли иск. He was sued. (A complaint was issued against him.)

иск-а́тель, searcher, seeker

Э́то настоя́щий иска́тель приключе́ний. He is a real adventurer.

иск-а́ть, to look for, search

Я ищу́ каранда́ш. I am looking for a pencil.

вз-ыск-а́тельный, strict, exacting

Вы сли́шком взыска́тельны. You are too exacting.

вз-ыск-а́ть(взъ-иск-ать), to exact, recover

Он взыска́л изде́ржки судо́м. He recovered costs in a suit at law.

из-ы́ск-анный, refined, dainty, artistic

У неё изы́сканный вкус. She has a refined taste.

об-ы́ск, search

Поли́ция де́лает о́быск. The police are making a search.

с-ы́щ-ик, detective

Сы́щик напа́л на след преступле́ния. The detective has come upon the clue of the crime.

К

КАЗ-, SEEM, APPEAR, EXPRESS

каз-а́ться, to seem, appear

Мне ка́жется что вы правы́. It seems to me that you are right.

ск-аз-а́ть, to tell

Скажи́те ему́ что я бу́ду его́ ждать. Tell him that I shall expect him.

с-каз-ка, fairy tale

Он любит сказки. He likes fairy tales.

выс-каз-аться, to say out, express

Дайте ему высказаться. Let him express himself.

на-каз, instruction, decree

Мы читали Наказ Екатерины Великой. We were reading the Instruction of Catherine the Great.

от-каз, refusal, denial, rejection

Они получили отказ. They were refused.

по-каз-ать, to show

Я покажу вам эту картину. I will show you this picture.

при-каз, order, command

Начальник отдаёт приказ. The chief is issuing an order.

рас-с-каз, story, tale

Рассказы Чехова интересны. Chekhov's stories are interesting.

у-каз-ать, to point, show

Укажите ему дорогу. Show him the way.

КАЗ-, PUNISH

каз-нить, to execute, put to death

Всех пятерых казнили. All five were put to death.

каз-нь, execution

Их приговорили к смертной казни. They were sentenced to death.

ис-каж-ать, ⎤
             ⎬ to distort, disfigure
ис-каз-ить, ⎦

Шрам исказил ему лицо. A scar disfigured his face.

Не искажайте истины. Don't distort the truth.

КАМ-, STONE, ROCK

кám-ень, stone, rock

Дéти бросáют кáмни. The children throw stones.

кáм-енный, stone

Он купил кáменный дом. He bought a stone house.

кам-енúстый, stony, rocky

Каменúстая пóчва. A rocky ground (soil).

кáм-енщик, mason, brick-layer

Мы не мóжем найтú кáменщика. We cannot find a bricklayer.

о-кам-енéть, to petrify

От стрáха онá окаменéла. She was petrified with fright.

КАТ-, ROLL, RIDE

кат-áться, to ride

Зимóй приятно катáться на санях. In winter it is pleasant to go sleigh riding.

кат-úть, to roll

Рабóчие катúли бóчку по мостовóй. The workmen were rolling a barrel on the road.

кат-óк, skating-rink

На каткé игрáла мýзыка. The band played on the skating-rink.

кат-ýшка, spool, reel

Принесúте мне катýшку нúток. Bring me a spool of thread.

кач-áть, to rock, swing, sway

Мать качáет ребёнка. The mother rocks the child.

кач-éли, swing

У нас в садý качéли. We have a swing in the garden.

кáч-ка, rolling, tossing, pitching

Матрóсы не боятся кáчки. The sailors are not afraid of rolling (and pitching).

за-ка́т, sunset

Они́ любова́лись зака́том со́лнца. They were admiring the sunset.

КИД-, TOSS

кид-а́ть, } to toss, fling, throw, pitch
ки́-нуть (кид-нуть), }

Ма́льчик ки́нул мяч. The boy pitched the ball.

вы-кид-ывать, to discard, dismiss, play tricks

Он лю́бит выки́дывать шу́тки. He likes to play tricks.

под-кид-ыш, foundling

На крыльце́ пла́кал под-ки́дыш. A foundling was wailing on the porch.

на-кид-ка, mantle, cloak, wrap

Ей привезли́ краси́вую наки́дку. They brought her a beautiful wrap.

с-кид-ка, discount, reduced price

Това́р здесь продаётся со ски́дкой. The merchandise is sold here at reduced prices.

о-про-кин-уть, to upset, tip over, overturn

Я опроки́нул стул. I tipped the chair over.

КИП-, BOIL

кип-е́ть, to boil, seethe

Вода́ в ча́йнике кипи́т. The water in the teapot is boiling.

кип-у́чий, intense, fervent

Нигде́ нет тако́й кипу́чей де́ятельности как в Аме́рике. There is nowhere else such an intense activity as in America.

кип-ято́к, boiling water

Он побежа́л за кипятко́м. He rushed to fetch the boiling water.

вс-кип-яти́ть, to boil

Вскипяти́те молоко́. Boil the milk.

КИС-, КВАС-, SOUR

кис-лотá, acid, acidity

Кислотý мóжно купи́ть в
апте́ке.   Acid may be
bought at the drug store.

ки́с-лый, sour

Я спеклá пирóг из ки́слых
я́блок. I made a pie with
sour apples.

ки́с-нуть (кисл-нуть), to get
sour, turn sour

Нáше винó ки́снет.   Our
wine is getting sour.

Не́чего сиде́ть дóма и ки́сн-
уть. You must not stay at
home and turn sour (stale).

кис-éль, jelly

Мы еди́м мали́новый кисéль.
We are eating raspberry
jelly.

квас, sour drink

Квас освежáющий напи́ток.
Kvass is a refreshing drink.

квáс-ить, to ferment, pickle

Крестья́нка собирáется квá-
сить капýсту. The peas-
ant woman is starting to
make sauerkraut.

КЛАД-, PUT, HIDE

клад, treasure

Говоря́т, что здесь спря́тан
клад.   They say that
treasure is hidden here.

клáд-бище, cemetery

Стóрож живёт óколо клáд-
бища. The watchman lives
near the cemetery.

клад-овáя, pantry

В кладовóй мнóго с'естны́х
припáсов. In the pantry
there are many food sup-
plies.

клас-ть (клад-ть), to put

Кудá вы кладёте кни́ги?
Where do you put the
books?

до-клáд-ывать, to report, announce, add — Секретáрь доклáдывает о положéнии дел. The secretary reports about the situation.

за-клáд, bet, wager, pledge, mortgage — Не стóит вам бúться об заклáд. You should not bet.

у-клáд-ываться, to lie down, to pack — Нам порá уклáдываться. It's time for us to pack.

КЛЕВ-, PECK

клёв, biting, peck — Поéдем удúть, сегóдня хорóший клёв. Let's go fishing, the fish are biting today.

клев-áть, to peck — Птúца клюёт зернó. The bird pecks the grain.

клюв, bill, beak — У воробья́ корóткий клюв. The sparrow has a short bill.

клю́-нуть, to bite — Ры́ба клю́нула. The fish are biting.

клев-етá, calumny, slander — От клеветы́ не уйдёшь. One cannot get away from slander.

клев-етáть, to slander, malign, cast aspersion — Зачéм вы на негó клевéщете? Why do you cast aspersion upon him?

клев-етнúк, slanderer — Он обозвáл дрýга клеветникóм. He called his friend a slanderer.

КЛИК-, КРИК-, CALL, CRY

клúк-ать, клúк-нуть, } to call — Клúкни егó! Call him.

клич, call, cry, shout — Раздáлся боевóй клич. The war cry sounded.

клич-ка, name, nickname

Знáет-ли попугáй свою клúчку? Does the parrot know his name?

пере-клúч-ка, roll call

Он не явúлся на переклúчку. He did not come to tho roll call.

крик, shout, cry, call, scream

На её крик прибежáла прислýга. Hearing her scream, the servants rushed in.

крик-ýн, noisy person, bawler

Крикýна увелú в учáсток. The bawler was taken to the police station.

крич-áть, to shout

Не кричúте пожáлуйста. Please don't shout.

вос-клиц-áние, exclamation

При её появлéнии раздáлись восклицáния. At her appearance exclamations were heard.

КЛИН-, КЛЯ-, OATH, CURSE, SWEAR

за-клин-áть, to conjure, implore

Мать заклинáла дочь не оставлять дóма. The mother implored her daughter not to leave her home.

про-клин-áть, to curse, rue

Онá проклинáет тот день когдá онá встрéтилась с нúми. She rues that day when she met them.

кля-сть, to curse

Он клянёт егó в душé. In his soul he curses him.

кля-тва, oath, vow

С меня взяли клятву. They made me swear (allegiance).

про-кля-тие, curse, imprecation

Из тюрьмы слышались проклятия. Curses reached us from the prison.

КЛОН-, КЛАН-, BEND, BOW

клон-и́ть, to lean, drive, incline

Не понима́ю, куда́ он кло́нит. I don't understand what he is driving at.

на-кло́н-ность, inclination, tendency

У него́ накло́нность к аза́ртной игре́. He has a tendency to gamble.

по-кло́н, greeting, salute, bow

Покло́н вам от всех. Greetings to you from all (of us).

по-кло́н-ник, admirer

Мой знако́мый покло́нник Толсто́го. An acquaintance of mine is an admirer of Tolstoy.

с-клон, slope, decline

На скло́не лет он заду́мал жени́ться. In his declining years he decided to get married.

с-клон-и́ть, to bend, stoop, win over

Нам удало́сь склони́ть его́ на на́шу сто́рону. We succeeded in winning him over to our side.

у-клон-е́ние, deviation, evasion

Это уклоне́ние от те́мы. This is a deviation from the topic.

клан-яться, to greet, bow, send one's respects

Кла́няйтесь ва́шей ма́тушке. Greet your mother. (Give my respects to your mother.)

рас-кла́н-иваться,
рас-кла́н-яться, } to bow, salute, take one's hat off

Они́ раскла́нялись и разошли́сь. They bowed and took leave.

КЛЮЧ-, KEY

ключ, key

Он потеря́л свой ключ. He lost his key.

ключ-ница, housekeeper

Мáрья Ивáновна былá у них ключницей. Maria Ivanovna was their house-keeper.

ключ-евóй, spout, spring

Ключевáя водá холоднá. Spring-water is cold.

вы́-ключ-ить, to turn off, switch off

У нас вы́ключили электричество. Our electricity was turned off.

за-ключ-éние, conclusion, deduction, imprisonment

Вáше заключéние вéрно. Your conclusion is correct.

ис-ключ-и́тельный, exceptional

Это исключи́тельный слýчай. This is an exceptional case.

КНИГ-, BOOK

кни́г-а, book

Чья это кни́га? Whose book is it?

кни́ж-ка, book

У меня́ нет записнóй кни́жки. I have no notebook.

кни́ж-ный, book

Зайдёмте в кни́жный магази́н. Let's go to the book-store.

КОВ-, FORGE, CONFINE

ков-áть, to forge, beat, strike

Куй желéзо покá горячó. Strike while the iron is hot.

на-ков-áльня, anvil

Кузнéц положи́л гвоздь на наковáльню. The black-smith put a nail on the anvil.

о-кóв-ы, fetters, shackles

Арестáнты позвя́кивали окóвами. The convicts clanked their fetters.

под-кóв-а, horseshoe

Лóшадь потеря́ла подкóву. The horse lost a shoe.

при-ков-а́ть, to chain, forge, confine

Боле́знь прикова́ла его́ к посте́ли. The illness confined him to his bed.

КОЖ-, SKIN, HIDE, LEATHER

ко́ж-а, skin, leather

Из ко́жи де́лают о́бувь. Footware is made of leather.

ко́ж-аный, leather

Носи́льщик несёт ко́жаный чемода́н. The porter carries a leather suitcase.

кож-е́венный, leather, hide, tannery

Он рабо́тает на коже́венном заво́де. He works at the tannery.

КОЗ-, GOAT

коз-а́, goat

Коза́ попа́ла в огоро́д. The goat got into the vegetable garden.

коз-ёл, goat

Я не хочу́ быть козло́м отпуще́ния. I do not want to be a scapegoat.

ко́з-ий, goat

До́ктор посове́товал пить ко́зье молоко́. The physician advised to drink goat milk.

ко́з-лы, box, coach-box

Ку́чер сиди́т на ко́злах. The driver is seated on the coach-box.

КОЛ-, POINT, PRICK, CIRCLE

кол, stake, pole, picket

От забо́ра оста́лся то́лько кол. Only a pole is left of the fence.

кол-есо́, wheel

Колесо́ слома́лось. The wheel broke.

кол-ея́, rut, track

На доро́ге видна́ колея́. A rut is running (is seen) along the road.

ко́л-кий, sharp, stinging

Произошёл ко́лкий разго-во́р. A sharp conversation took place.

кол-о́ть, to stab, thrust, sting

У него́ коло́ло в боку́. He had a stabbing (sharp) pain in his side.

кол-ь-цо́, ring

На её па́льце обруча́льное кольцо́. There is a wedding ring on her finger.

рас-ко́л, split, schism

Но́вое уче́ние привело́ к раско́лу. The new teaching brought about a schism.

о́-кол-о, near

Они́ живу́т о́коло нас. They live near us.

о-ко́л-ь-ный, roundabout

Мы прие́хали в дере́вню око́льным путём. We came to the village by a roundabout road.

КОЛ-, WAVER

кол-еба́ть, to sway, waver, agitate, vibrate

Ве́тер коле́блет жа́тву. The wind sways the crop.

кол-еба́ние, fluctuation, oscillation

Здесь ре́зкое колеба́ние температу́ры. There is a sharp fluctuation of temperature here.

кол-ыбе́ль, cradle

Ребёнок спит в колыбе́ли. The child sleeps in the cradle.

КОН-, BEGINNING, END

ис-кон-и́, from time immemorial, from the very beginning

Искони́ так ведётся. It has been established so from the very beginning.

кон-е́ц, end, termination

В конце́ концо́в он согла-
си́лся со мной. Finally
(at last) he agreed with me.

кон-е́чно, certainly, of course

Вы коне́чно зае́дете к нам.
Of course you will call
on us.

ко́н-чить, to end, finish, complete

Мы ко́нчили рабо́ту. We
have finished our work.

за-ка́н-чивать, to finish, complete, conclude

Мы зака́нчиваем пе́рвую
часть уче́бника. We are
finishing the first part of
the textbook.

за-ко́н, law

Вы́шел но́вый зако́н об ино-
стра́нцах. A new law was
issued concerning for-
eigners.

за-ко́н-ный, lawful, legal,
rightful, just

Э́то зако́нное тре́бование.
This demand is lawful.
This is a just demand.

о-кон-ча́ние, end, ending,
completion

Ещё час до оконча́ния спек-
та́кля. We still have an
hour before the end of the
play.

КОН-, HORSE

кон-ёк, fad, hobby

Э́то его́ конёк. This is his
hobby.

ко́н-ница, cavalry

Ко́нница мча́лась во весь
опо́р. The cavalry rushed
at full speed.

ко́н-ный, horse, mounted

Ко́нный отря́д отпра́вился к
грани́це. The mounted
troops started towards the
border.

кон-ь, horse

У казака́ укра́ли коня́. The
Cossack's horse was stolen.

кóн-юх, groom, stableman	Кóнюх смóтрит за лошадьми́. The groom looks after the horses.
кон-ю́шня, stable	Из коню́шни слы́шалось ржа́ние лошаде́й. One could hear the neighing of the horses in the stable.

КОП-, DIG, PIERCE

коп-áть, to dig	Я копа́ю зéмлю. I am digging the ground.
коп-ьё, lance, bayonet	Они́ би́лись на кóпьях. (They were tilting). They were fighting with bayonets.
о-кóп-ы, trenches	Солда́ты рóют окóпы. The soldiers are digging the trenches.

КОП-, КУП-, SAVE, HEAP, BUY

коп-éйка, copeck	Да́йте ма́льчику копéйку. Give the boy a copeck.
коп-и́ть, to save	Они́ кóпят дéньги на чёрный день. They are saving the money for a rainy day.
коп-на́, rick, stack	Сéно сóбрано в копну́. The hay is gathered into a rick.
ку́ч-а, heap, pile	На дворé лежи́т ку́ча му́сору. A pile of rubbish lies in the yard.
вы́-куп, ransom	За негó да́ли большóй вы́куп. They paid for him a big ransom.
за-ку́п-щик, buyer	Заку́пщиков посла́ли заграни́цу. The buyers were sent abroad.

куп-е́ц, merchant

Купе́ц стои́т за прила́вком. The merchant stands behind the counter.

куп-е́чество, merchants, mercantile class

Мно́го писа́ли о ру́сском купе́честве. A great deal was written about the Russian merchants.

куп-и́ть, to buy

Я куплю́ всё необходи́мое. I shall buy all that is necessary.

под-куп-и́ть, to bribe

Э́того чино́вника ниче́м не подку́пишь. There is nothing with which you could bribe this official.

по-куп-а́ть, to buy, purchase

Не покупа́йте в э́том магази́не. Don't buy in this store.

по-ку́п-ка, purchase

Вот моя́ поку́пка. Here is my purchase.

с-куп-о́й, stingy

Он о́чень скуп. He is very stingy.

КОР-, REPROACH, GAIN, SUBJECT

кор-и́ть, to reproach, blame

В глаза́ не хвали́, за глаза́ не кори́. Don't flatter to one's face, don't blame behind one's back.

кор-ы́сть, cupidity, gain, profit, selfishness

Он всё де́лает из коры́сти. Everything he does is prompted by his cupidity.

по-кор-и́ть, to subject, conquer

Наполео́н покори́л всю Евро́пу. Napoleon conquered entire Europe.

у-ко́р, reproach

Она́ смо́трит на меня́ с уко́ром. She looks at me reproachfully.

КОР-, ROOT

кор-еннóй, radical, native, fundamental

Кореннóе населéние здесь рýсское. Here the native population is Russian.

кóр-ень, root

Кóрни дýба идýт глубокó в зéмлю. The roots of an oak go deep into the ground.

кор-ешóк, root, back

Корешóк словаря пóрван. The back of the dictionary is torn.

кор-ѝца, cinnamon

Положѝте кусóк корѝцы в рис. Add a piece of cinnamon to the rice.

ис-кор-еня́ть, } to eradicate,
ис-кор-енѝть, } destroy

Мéра э́та искоренѝла мнóго злоупотреблéний. This measure eradicated many abuses.

КОРМ-, FOOD, FEED

корм, food, fodder

Заготóвьте корм для скотá. Get the fodder ready for the cattle.

корм-ѝлица, wet nurse

Онѝ наняли кормѝлицу. They hired a wet nurse.

корм-ѝть, to feed, nourish, board

В áрмии хорошó кóрмят. They give good food in the army. (The army is well fed.)

КОС-, ЧЕС-, TRESS, COMB

кос-á, plait, braid

У неё длѝнная косá. She has a long braid.

кос-мáтый, dishevelled

Он всегдá космáтый. He is always dishevelled.

чес-áть, to scratch, comb

Мужи́к чéшет заты́лок. **The peasant scratches the back of his head.**

чес-óтка, itch

От чесóтки трýдно избáвиться. It is difficult to get rid of an itch.

при-чёс-ка, headdress, coiffure

У вас краси́вая причёска. Your headdress is becoming (beautiful).

при-чёс-ываться, to comb

Я причёсываюсь пéред зéркалом. I comb (my hair) in front of a mirror.

КОС-, SCYTHE, CUT

кос-á, scythe

Лéзвие косы́ острó. The blade of a scythe is sharp.

кóс-арь, mower, haymaker

Косари́ ужé давнó на лугý. The peasant mowers have already been in the meadow for a long time.

кос-и́ть, to mow, cut

Они́ кóсят травý. They are mowing the grass.

КОСТ-, BONE

кост-ь, bone

Эта корóбка сдéлана из кóсти. This box is made of bone.

кост-ля́вый, bony

У старýх рýки костля́вы. Old women's hands are bony.

кост-ы́ль, crutch

Он урони́л свой косты́ль. He dropped his crutch.

кос-нéть (кост-неть), to stagnate, become stale

В провинции лю́ди нерéдко коснéют. In the province the people often stagnate.

КРАД-, STEAL

крас-ть (крад-ть), to steal

> Одни́ краду́т, а други́е пря́чут. Some steal while others hide (the stolen goods).

кра́ж-а, theft

> Их обвини́ли в кра́же. They were accused of theft.

в-кра́д-чивый, insinuating, oily, smooth, coaxing

> Она́ говори́ла вкра́дчивым го́лосом. She spoke in a coaxing voice.

в-кра́д-ываться, to steal in, slip in, creep in

> При перепи́ске вкра́дываются оши́бки. Mistakes creep in while copying.

КРАС-, BEAUTY

крас-и́вый, beautiful, handsome

> У вас краси́вая ме́бель. You have beautiful furniture.

кра́с-ить, to paint

> Маля́р кра́сит забо́р. The painter paints the fence.

крас-ота́, beauty

> Я преклоня́юсь пе́ред красото́й приро́ды. I worship the beauty of nature.

кра́с-ный, red

> Оши́бки испра́влены кра́сными черни́лами. The mistakes are corrected in red ink.

у-краш-а́ть, to beautify, decorate, adorn, trim

> Де́ти украша́ют ёлку. The children are decorating the Christmas tree.

КРАТ-, КОРОТ-, SHORT, BRIEF

кра́т-кий, short, brief

> Мы шли кра́тким путём. We took a short cut.

кра́т-кость, brevity, shortness

> Его́ речь хвали́ли за кра́ткость. His speech was praised for its brevity.

пре-крат-и́ть, to cease, put an end, stop

Прошу́ прекрати́ть э́тот раз-гово́р. I beg you to stop this conversation.

со-кращ-а́ть, ⎱ to shorten,
со-крат-и́ть, ⎰ curtail

Нам необходи́мо сократи́ть расхо́ды. We must curtail our expenses.

По суббо́там сокраща́ют рабо́-чие часы́. On Saturdays they shorten the working hours.

корот-а́ть, to spend time, kill time

По́мните, как мы с ва́ми корота́ли вечера́. Do you remember how we used to pass the evenings?

коро́т-кий, short

У него́ коро́ткие но́ги. He has short legs.

КРЕП-, (КРѢП)-, STRONG

крѐп-кий, strong, firm, ro-bust, vigorous

У него́ крѐпкое здоро́вье. His health is robust.

крѐп-нуть, to get stronger, get firmer

Лёд на реке́ крѐпнет. The ice on the river is getting firmer.

креп-остни́чество, serfdom

Наста́л коне́ц крепостни́че-ству́. Serfdom came to an end.

крѐп-ость, fortress

Престу́пника заточи́ли в крѐ-пость. The criminal was imprisoned in the fortress.

у-креп-ле́ние, fortification

У вхо́да в га́вань постро́или укрепле́ние. They erected a fortification at the entrance to the harbor.

КРЕСТ-, КРЕС-, CROSS

крест, cross

Крест си́мвол христиа́нства. The cross is the symbol of Christianity.

крест-и́ть, to baptize

Его́ крести́ли в це́ркви. He was baptized in church.

крест-о́вый, crusader, cross-bearing

Ры́цари уча́ствовали в кре-сто́вых похо́дах. The knights participated in the crusades.

крест-ь-я́нин, peasant

Крестья́не па́шут и се́ют. The peasants plough and sow.

крещ-е́ние, baptism, christen-ing

Он при́нял креще́ние. He was baptized.

вос-крес-а́ть, вос-кре́с-нуть,} to rise from the dead, revive

Христо́с воскре́с! Christ is risen!

вос-крес-е́нье, Sunday

В воскресе́нье у нас бы́ло мно́го госте́й. On Sunday we had many visitors.

вос-креш-а́ть, вос-крес-и́ть, } to resurrect, revive

Они́ воскреша́ют ста́рые оббы́-чаи. They resurrect the old customs.

КРОВ-, BLOOD

кров-а́вый, bloody, blood-stained

Ра́неный зверь оста́вил кро-ва́вый след. The wounded animal left a bloody trail.

кро́в-ный, blood-relation, deadly

Ему́ нанесли́ кро́вную оби́ду. They hurled a deadly insult at him. They deeply insulted him.

кров-ь, blood

Э́то у него́ в крови́. It runs in his blood.

кров-о-жа́дность, blood-thirstiness

В кровожа́дности он не уступа́ет хи́щному зве́рю. In bloodthirstiness he matches a wild animal.

КРОХ-, CRUMB, SMALL PIECE

кро́х-а, crumb

От их состоя́ния оста́лись то́лько кро́хи. From their fortune there remained a few crumbs.

кро́х-отный, tiny

У неё кро́хотная ру́чка. She has a tiny hand.

кро́ш-ка, mite, little one, baby

Он совсе́м ещё кро́шка у вас. Your child is still a baby.

крош-и́ть, to crumble

Стари́к кро́шит хлеб в суп. The old man crumbles some bread into his soup.

КРУГ-, CIRCLE, SPHERE, ROUND

круг, circle

У меня́ большо́й круг зна-ко́мых. I have a large circle of friends.

кру́г-лый, round, entire

Они́ живу́т кру́глый год в дере́вне. They live in the country all the year round.

кру́ж-ево, lace

На ней то́нкое кру́жево. She is wearing a fine lace.

круж-и́ть, to circle

Орёл кружи́т в облака́х. The eagle circles among the clouds.

кру́ж-ка, cup, jug

Ему́ по́дали кру́жку воды́. They gave him a cup of water.

о-круж-а́ть, } to surround
о-круж-и́ть, }

Толпа́ дете́й окружи́ла учи́-теля. A crowd of children surrounded their teacher.

КРЫ-, КРОВ-, SHELTER, COVER

кры-ть, to cover	В э́той дере́вне и́збы кры́ты соло́мой. In this village the huts are covered with straw.
кры́ш-а, roof	У них протека́ет кры́ша. Their roof is leaking.
от-кры́-тие, discovery	Об э́том откры́тии мно́го писа́ли. Much has been written about this discovery.
от-кры-ва́ть, to open	Не открыва́йте окна́. Do not open the window.
по-кры-ва́ло, cover, spread	На посте́ли бе́лое покрыва́ло. A white spread was on the bed.
с-кры́-ть, to cover up, hide, conceal	Он скрыл следы́ преступле́ния. He concealed the traces of the crime.
кров, shelter	Она́ оста́лась без кро́ва. She was left without shelter.
от-кров-е́нность, frankness	Открове́нность вызыва́ет дове́рие. Frankness inspires one with confidence.
по-кров-и́тельствовать, to protect, patronize	Нача́льник ему́ покрови́тельствует. His chief patronizes him.
со-кров-е́нный, secret, innermost	Вы угада́ли мои́ сокрове́нные мы́сли. You have guessed my innermost thoughts.
со-кро́в-ище, treasure	Госуда́рственные сокро́вища храня́тся в подземе́льи. The state treasures are kept in an underground vault.

КУП-, BATHE

куп-а́льня, bathers' booth

Мы раздева́емся в купа́льне. We are undressing in the bathers' booth.

куп-а́нье, bathing

Морски́е купа́нья поле́зны. Sea bathing is wholesome.

куп-а́ть, to bathe

Она́ купа́ет младе́нца. She is bathing an infant.

вы́-куп-аться, to bathe, to take a plunge

Ле́том прия́тно вы́купаться в реке́. In summer it is pleasant to take a plunge (bathe) in the river.

КУС-, BITE, TASTE

кус-а́ть, to bite

От зло́сти он куса́л гу́бы. He was biting his lips in anger.

кус-о́к, piece, slice

Да́йте ему́ кусо́к хле́ба. Give him a slice of bread.

ку́ш-ать, to eat

Ку́шайте на здоро́вье. Eat, it is good for you (your health).

у-кус-и́ть, to bite

Соба́ка укуси́ла де́вочку. The dog bit the little girl.

в-кус, taste

На вкус и на цвет това́рища нет. Every one has his own taste.

в-ку́с-ный, tasty

По́дали вку́сное блю́до. A tasty dish was served.

за-ку́с-ка, relish

Заку́ска на столе́. The relishes are on the table.

ис-ку́с-ство, art

Мы интересу́емся иску́сством. We are interested in art.

ис-куш-éние, temptation

Это большóе искушéние. This is a great temptation.

по-куш-éние, attempt

На губернáтора бы́ло покушéние. An attempt was made on the governor's life.

рас-кус-и́ть, to bite in two, understand, grasp

Егó трýдно раскуси́ть. It is hard to understand him.

КУТ-, WRAP, MUFFLE, TWIST

кýт-ать, to wrap, muffle

Бáба кýтает гóлову платкóм. The peasant woman wraps her head in a kerchief.

за-кýт-ываться, to wrap up, muffle, dress

Зимóй лю́ди закýтываются в тёплые одéжды. In winter people (are wearing) wear warm clothes. (In winter the people are muffled in warm clothes.)

кут-ёж, spree, carouse, revelry

Кутёж продолжáлся до утрá. The revelry lasted until morning.

кут-ерьмá, commotion, row

Там поднялáсь стрáшная кутерьмá. A terrible commotion started there.

кут-и́ть, to make merry, to be on a spree

Всю ночь они́ кути́ли. They were on a spree all night.

Л

ЛАД-, HARMONY

лад, harmony, concern, accord

Дéло идёт на лад. Things are getting along.

лáд-ить, to get along

Они́ не лáдят мéжду собóй. They don't get along.

раз-лáд, discord

Онá повсю́ду внóсит разлáд. She brings discord everywhere.

у-ла́ж-ивать, ⎰ to arrange,   Не беспоко́йтесь, я всё
у-ла́д-ить, ⎱ settle, уложу́. Don't worry, I'll
               make up settle everything. (Don't
worry, I'll arrange every-
thing.)

ЛАСК-, CARESS, CLING

ла́ск-а, caress, kindness — В её глаза́х све́тит ла́ска. Kindness shines in her eyes.

ласк-а́ть, to caress, pet, fondle — Ма́льчик ласка́ет ко́шку. The boy pets the cat.

ла́ск-овый, kind, affectionate — Он при́нял меня́ ла́сково. He received (met) me affectionately.

ла́ст-ить, to fawn, flatter — В ожида́нии насле́дства он ла́стит старику́. He fawns upon the old man, expecting to get an inheritance from him.

ЛГ-, ЛОЖ-, LIE, DECEIT

лг-ать, to deceive, lie — Я не лгу. I am not deceiving.
лг-ун, liar — Он невыноси́мый лгун. He is an unspeakable liar.

лже-учи́тель, false teacher — Лжеучи́тель искажа́ет и́стину. A false teacher distorts the truth.

лж-и́вый, false, deceitful — Лжи́вому не верь. Don't trust a deceitful person.

ло́ж-ный, false — В газе́те появи́лись ло́жные слу́хи. False rumors appeared in the newspaper.

лож-ь, lie — Э́то про́сто ложь. This is simply a lie.

ЛЕГ-, ЛАГ-, ЛОГ-, LIE, DOWN, PUT

леч-ь (лег-ть), to lie down

Мы легли́ спать ра́но. We went to bed early.

на-лег-а́ть, to lean on, to drink or eat heartily

Не налега́й на вино́. Don't drink too much wine.

на-лаг-а́ть, } **to impose, put
на-лож-и́ть,** } **on, lay on**

Она́ гото́ва наложи́ть на себя́ ру́ки. She is ready to commit suicide.

по-лаг-а́ть, to think, deem, suppose

Я полага́ю что он за́втра бу́дет здесь. I suppose he will be here tomorrow.

от-лож-и́ть, to postpone, put off

Нам пришло́сь отложи́ть пое́здку. We had to postpone our trip.

леж-а́ть, to lie

Я лежу́ в посте́ли. I am (lying) in bed.

при-над-леж-а́ть, to belong

Кому́ принадлежи́т э́тот слова́рь? To whom does this dictionary belong?

при-ле́ж-ный, industrious, diligent

Ваш брат приле́жный учени́к. Your brother is an industrious pupil.

на-ло́г, tax

В э́том году́ нало́ги высоки́. This year the taxes are high.

пред-ло́г, pretext, pretence, excuse

Он не пришёл под предло́гом боле́зни. He did not come under pretext of illness.

пред-лож-е́ние, proposal, suggestion, offer

Ва́ше предложе́ние при́нято. Your offer is accepted.

до-лож-и́ть, to report, add

Позво́льте вам доложи́ть о происше́ствии. Let me report about the accident.

ЛЕГ-, ЛЕЗ-, ЛЬЗ-, EASE, BENEFIT, USE

лёг-кий, easy

Лёгкий уро́к. An easy lesson.

об-лег-че́ние, relief

Лека́рство не принесло́ облегче́ния. The medicine did not bring any relief.

об-лег-ча́ть, ⎰ to lighten, re-
об-лег-чи́ть, ⎱ lieve, facilitate

Я стара́лся облегчи́ть ему́ рабо́ту. I tried to lighten (facilitate) his work for him.

по-ле́з-ный, useful

Ра́дио поле́зное изобре́тение. Radio is a useful invention.

не-льз-я́, impossible, one must not, one cannot

Вам нельзя́ кури́ть. You must not smoke.

по́-льз-а, profit, benefit, use, good

Кака́я от э́того по́льза? What good will it do?

по́-льз-оваться, to use, make use

Он по́льзуется мои́ми запи́сками. He is using my notes.

вос-по́-льз-оваться, to take advantage

Я воспо́льзуюсь э́тим слу́чаем. I shall take advantage of this opportunity.

ЛЕЗ-, (ЛѢЗ)-, ЛАЗ, ЛЗ-, CLIMB, COME OUT

лез-ть, to climb

Не лезь на де́рево. Don't climb up the tree.

ла́з-ить, to climb, clamber

Де́ти ла́зили по кры́ше. The children clambered up the roof.

водо-ла́з, diver

Водола́з опусти́лся на дно. The diver sank to the bottom.

ле́с-тница, ladder

Он подня́лся по ле́стнице. He climbed the ladder.

по́-лз-ать, to crawl, creep

Змея́ по́лзает по земле́. The snake crawls on the ground.

вы́-по-лз-ти, to come out, crawl out

Ули́тка вы́ползла на тро-пи́нку. The snail crawled on the pathway.

ЛЕК-, (ЛѢК)-, CURE

лек-а́рство, remedy, medicine

Како́е го́рькое лека́рство. What bitter medicine!

ле́к-арь, surgeon, doctor

За ле́карем уже́ посла́ли. They have already sent for the doctor.

леч-е́бница, hospital

В лече́бнице мно́го больны́х. There are many patients in the hospital.

леч-е́ние, cure, treatment

Она́ уе́хала в Крым на лече́ние. She went to Crimea to take the cure.

леч-и́ть, to doctor, have treatments

Меня́ до́лго лечи́ли. They doctored me for a long time.

за-ле́ч-ивать, to heal

Вре́мя зале́чивает ра́ны. Time heals all wounds.

ЛЕС-, (ЛѢС)-, WOOD

лес, forest, woods

Пойдёмте в лес за я́годами. Let's go to the woods berry hunting.

лес-ни́к, forester, ranger

У овра́га жил лесни́к. The forester lived near the ravine.

лес-ни́чий, forester

Он занима́л ме́сто лесни́чего. He had the position of a forester. (He was employed as a forester.)

лес-но́й, woods, woodland

Худо́жник рисова́л лесно́й пейза́ж. The artist was painting a woodland scene.

лес-о-пи́лка, sawmill

Оте́ц рабо́тает на лесопи́лке. Father works in the sawmill.

ле́ш-ий, wood-demon

Когда́-то ве́рили в ле́ших. Long ago people believed in wood-demons.

ЛЕТ-, FLY

лет, flying, in the air

Он подхвати́л мяч на лету́. He caught the ball in the air.

лет-а́ть, }to fly
лет-е́ть, }

Пти́цы лета́ют по во́здуху. Birds fly in the air.

Вон гу́си летя́т. Look, the geese are flying there.

лёт-чик, aviator

Никола́й о́пытный лётчик. Nicholas is an experienced aviator.

на-лёт, raid, inroad

Налёт ко́нницы причини́л мно́го вреда́. The cavalry raid has done much damage.

по-лёт, flight, flying

Мы смо́трим на полёт аэропла́на. We watch the flight (course) of an airplane.

ЛИ-, POUR

ли́-вень, downpour

Како́й сего́дня ли́вень! What a downpour we have today!

ли-ть, to pour, rain

С утра́ льёт дождь. It has rained since morning.

раз-ли-ва́ть, to pour

Она́ разлива́ет чай. She pours the tea.

в-ли-ва́ть, to pour into

Я вливаю во́ду в скля́нку. I am pouring water into a flask.

в-ли-я́ние, influence, authority

Сове́т мой оказа́л влия́ние на него́. My advice has had an influence on him.

в-ли-я́ть, to influence

Воспита́тель влия́ет на дете́й. A tutor influences the children

за-ли́-в, gulf, bay

В зали́ве виднёется парохо́д. A steamer is seen on the bay.

про-ли́-в, strait, sound

В проли́ве нас засти́гла бу́ря. A storm overtook us in the sound.

на-ли́-вка, cordial

Попро́буйте вишнёвую нали́вку. Try the cherry cordial.

с-ли́-вки, cream

Мы пьём ко́фе со сли́вками. We drink coffee with cream.

ЛИК-, FACE

лик, face, countenance

Из ико́ны гляде́ли ли́ки святы́х. The faces of the saints looked down from the ikons.

лиц-еме́рие, hypocrisy

Лицеме́рие э́того скря́ги изве́стно. The hypocrisy of this miser is well known.

лиц-о́, face, countenance

Я встре́тился с ним лицо́м к лицу́. I ran into him. (I met him face to face.)

ли́ч-ность, individual, person

Что э́то за ли́чность? Who is this? (What sort of person is he?)

раз-лич-а́ть, to discern, make out — В темноте́ я не различа́ю кто там. In the darkness I cannot make out who is there.

с-лич-а́ть, to compare, collate — Нота́риус слича́ет докуме́нты. The attorney compares the documents.

у-ли́к-а, evidence, proof — Э́та вещь послу́жит ули́кой. This object will serve as evidence.

ЛИХ-, ЛИШ-, EVIL, SUPERFLUOUS

лих-о́й, evil, wicked, cruel, bold — Пришла́ лиха́я беда́. A cruel misfortune came (upon us).

лиш-а́ть,⎱ to deprive, rob,
лиш-и́ть,⎰ deny — Не лиша́йте нас удово́льствия пообе́дать с на́ми. Don't deprive us of the pleasure of having you to dinner.

ли́ш-ний, superfluous — Мно́го писа́ли о ли́шних лю́дях. Much was written about superfluous people.

с-ли́ш-ком, too — Здесь сли́шком жа́рко. It is too hot here.

ЛУГ-, MEADOW

луг, meadow — На лугу́ мно́го цвето́в. There are many flowers on the meadow.

луж-а́йка, grass-plot, little meadow — Пе́ред ро́щей зелёная лужа́йка. There is a little meadow in front of the grove.

ЛУК-, BOW, BEND, PART

лук, bow

Стрела́ из лу́ка попа́ла в цель. The arrow from the bow hit the mark.

лук-а́вый, sly, cunning

У неё лука́вые глаза́. She has a sly look in her eyes.

раз-лу́к-а, separation, parting

Мы встре́тились по́сле до́лгой разлу́ки. We met after a long separation.

раз-луч-а́ться, to part, separate

Э́ти сёстры никогда́ не разлуча́ются. These sisters never part.

ЛЮБ-, LOVE

люб-е́зность, kindness, courtesy

Благодарю́ за ва́шу любе́зность. Thank you for your kindness.

люб-и́тель, lover, amateur, layman

Он большо́й люби́тель старины́. He is a great lover of antiquity.

люб-и́тельский, amateur, amateurish

Сего́дня люби́тельский спекта́кль. An amateur play is (to be given) today.

люб-и́ть, to love, like

Я люблю́ пе́ние. I like singing.

люб-ова́ться, to admire

Чем вы любу́етесь? What are you admiring?

люб-о́вь, love

Покоря́й сердца́ любо́вью, а не стра́хом. Conquer hearts with love and not with fear.

люб-о́й, any, whichever one likes

Возьми́те любо́й кусо́к. Take whatever piece you like.

раз-люб-и́ть, to become indifferent, to cease to love

Она́ ско́ро разлюби́ла его́. She soon became indifferent to him.

ЛЮД-, PEOPLE

люд-и, people

> Что э́то за лю́ди? Who are these people? (What sort of people are they?)

люд-о-е́д, cannibal

> Людое́ды существу́ют и тепе́рь. Cannibals exist (may be found) even now.

люд-ско́й, people's, popular

> От людско́й молвы́ ча́сто страда́ют. One often suffers from people's talk (from gossip).

много-лю́д-ный, crowded

> Он вошёл в многолю́дный храм. He walked into a crowded temple.

не-люд-и́мка, unsociable person, recluse

> Вы совсе́м преврати́лись в нелюди́мку. You have become a veritable recluse

M
МАЗ-, МАС-, DAUB, OIL, GREASE

ма́з-ать, to daub, smear

> Мужи́к ма́жет колесо́ дёгтем. The peasant smears the wheel with tar.

маз-ня́, daub

> Э́то не карти́на, а мазня́. It is not a painting, but a daub.

маз-ь, ointment, liniment, grease

> Не забу́дьте купи́ть ма́зи. Don't forget to buy the liniment for me.

за-ма́з-ка, putty

> Куда́ вы де́ли зама́зку? What did you do with the putty?

ма́с-леница, Shrovetide, carnival

> На ма́сленице едя́т блины́. At Shrovetide pancakes are eaten.

ма́с-ло, butter

> Я ем хлеб с ма́слом. I eat bread with butter.

мас-ло-бойка, churn

Хозяйка купила маслобойку. The housewife bought a churn.

МАЛ-, SMALL, LITTLE

мал-енький, small, little

Мы пили кофе из маленьких чашек. We drank coffee out of small cups.

мал-ый, fellow, lad, chap

Ваш друг добрый малый. Your friend is a kind-hearted fellow.

мал-ыш, small child, mite, tot

Её малыш шалун. Her tot is a mischievous child.

мал-ь-чик, boy

Мальчик продаёт газеты. The boy sells newspapers.

мал-ютка, baby, mite, tot

По улице шёл малютка. A tot was walking on the street.

мал-о-душный, fainthearted

Он малодушный человек. He is a fainthearted man.

МАХ-, WAVE, SLIP

мах, slip, in an instant, mistake

Он не даст маху. He won't let the opportunity slip. He won't make a mistake.

мах-ать, to wave

Она махала платком из окна. She waved her handkerchief from the window.

вз-мах, stroke, sweep

Одним взмахом он убил быка. At one stroke he killed the bull.

за-мах-нуться, to lift, raise, brandish

Офицер замахнулся саблей. The officer raised his sword.

про-мах, miss, slip, blunder, oversight

Вы стреляете без промаха. You shoot (and) never miss (the mark).

МГ-, МИГ-, ЖМ-, TWINKLE, WINK, BLINK

мг-новéние, instant, moment

Лунá показáлась на мгновéние. The moon appeared for a moment.

миг, (in) the twinkling of an eye, instant

Воображéние мѝгом перенеслó меня в Москвý. Instantly my imagination carried me to Moscow.

миг-áть, to wink

Перестáньте мигáть! Stop winking!

жм-ýриться, to blink

Кот жмýрится на сóлнце. The cat blinks in the sun.

жм-ýрки, blindman's buff

Дéти игрáют в жмýрки. The children are playing blindman's buff.

МЕЖ-, МЕЖД-, BOUNDARY, BETWEEN, INTER-

меж-á, bound, strip

Крестьянин полóл межý. The peasant was weeding the strip (of land).

мéжд-у, between, among

Мéжду нáми говоря. Speaking between ourselves.

межд-у-нарóдный, international

Междунарóдный конгрéсс собрáлся в Женéве. The international congress met in Geneva.

меж-евáть, to measure, survey, divide into lots

Онѝ межевáли зéмлю. They were dividing the land into lots.

про-меж-ýток, interval, span space

Я мнóго сдéлал в корóткий промежýток. I have done a great deal in a short time.

МЕК-, HINT, DREAM

на-мёк, hint, allusion

Ваш намёк слишком про-зрачен. Your hint is too obvious.

на-мек-а́ть, to hint

Я напра́сно намека́л ему́ о до́лге. In vain did I hint to him about his debt.

с-мек-а́ть, ⎱ to understand,
с-мек-ну́ть, ⎰ grasp

Он смекну́л в чём де́ло. He understood what the matter was.

меч-та́, dream, wish

Моя́ мечта́ пое́хать загра-ни́цу. My dream is to go abroad.

меч-та́ть, to dream

О чём вы мечта́ете? What are you dreaming about?

меч-та́тельный, dreamy

Она́ смотре́ла на зака́т меч-та́тельным взгля́дом. She was looking at the sunset with dreamy eyes.

МЕН-, (МѢН)-, CHANGE

мен-я́ть, to change, exchange

Я иду́ в банк меня́ть де́ньги. I am going to the bank to change some money.

вза-ме́н, in exchange, instead

Взаме́н де́нег ему́ да́ли това́р. In exchange for his money they gave him the goods.

из-мен-я́ть. ⎱ to change,
из-мен-и́ть. ⎰ betray

Шпио́н измени́л оте́честву. The spy betrayed his fatherland.

пере-ме́н-а, change

В конто́ре больша́я переме́на. There is a great change in the office.

раз-мен-я́ть, to change money

Ему́ пришло́сь разменя́ть сторублёвку. He had to change a hundred-rouble note.

с-мен-и́ть, to replace, relieve | Нас смени́ло молодо́е поколе́ние. The young generation replaced us.

МЕР-, МИР-, МОР-, DIE

мёр-твый, dead | Чита́ли-ли вы "Запи́ски из Мёртвого До́ма"? Have you read the "Memoirs from the House of Death"?

с-мёр-тный, mortal | Все мы сме́ртны. We are all mortal.

с-мер-ть, death | Он у́мер наси́льственной сме́ртью. He died a violent death.

у-мир-а́ть, to die | Больно́й умира́ет. The patient is dying.

мор-и́ть, to starve, famish, exhaust | Пле́нников мори́ли го́лодом. The prisoners were being starved.

об-мор-ок, fainting, swoon | Она́ упа́ла в о́бморок. She swooned.

МЕР-, (МѢР)-, MEASURE

ме́р-а, measure | Прими́те реши́тельные ме́ры про́тив ста́чечников. Take decisive measures against the strikers.

ме́р-ить, to measure | Вся́кий ме́рит на свой арши́н. Everyone measures with his own yardstick.

на-ме́р-ение, intention | У меня́ не́ было наме́рения оби́деть вас. I had no intention of offending you.

при-ме́р, example | Вот вам хоро́ший приме́р. Here is a good example for you.

при-мер-я́ть, to try on	Да́ма примеря́ет пла́тье. **The** lady is trying on a dress.
раз-ме́р, size	Како́го разме́ра ва́ши боти́нки? **What size are your** shoes?
у-ме́р-енный, temperate, moderate	В Калифо́рнии уме́ренный кли́мат. The climate in California is moderate.

МЕРЗ-, МОРОЗ-, COLD, FROST

мёрз-нуть, to be cold, freeze	Я мёрз всю зи́му. I froze all winter.
за-мерз-а́ть, to freeze	Вода́ замерза́ет в лу́же. The water in the puddle is freezing.
моро́з, frost, cold	Како́й вчера́ был моро́з! How bitterly cold it **was** yesterday!
моро́з-ить, to freeze	На дворе́ моро́зит. Outside it is freezing.
моро́ж-еное, ice cream	На сла́дкое по́дали моро́женое. For dessert they served ice cream.

МЕРК-, МРАК-, DARK

ме́рк-нуть, to grow dark, fade	День ме́ркнет. It is getting dark. (The day is fading.)
мерц-а́ть, to gleam, flicker	На тёмном не́бе мерца́ют звёзды. The stars flicker in the dark sky.
с-мерк-а́ться, to grow dark	Уже́ смерка́ется. Darkness is already falling. (It is already getting dark.)

мрак, darkness

В глуши́ цари́т мрак неве́-
жества.   The darkness of
ignorance reigns in the
backwoods.

мра́ч-ный, sombre, gloomy

Отчего́ вы тако́й мра́чный?
Why are you so gloomy?

МЕС-, (МѢС)-, MIX, KNEAD, DISTURB

мес-и́ть, to knead, mix

Пора́ меси́ть те́сто для
пирога́.   It's time to knead
the dough for the pie.

меш-а́ть, to disturb, hinder

Пожа́луйста не меша́йте мне.
Please do not disturb me.

в-меш-а́тельство, interference, meddling

Мы обойдёмся без вмеша́-
тельства посторо́нних. We
can get along without the
interference of strangers.

по-ме́х-а, hindrance, handicap

Плохо́е зре́ние ему́ больша́я
поме́ха.   His poor eyesight
is a great handicap to him.

с-мес-ь, mixture, concoction

Он пьёт каку́ю-то смесь. He
is drinking a concoction of
some kind.

МЕСТ-, (МѢСТ)-, PLACE

ме́ст-о, place, seat

Уступи́те ей ва́ше ме́сто.
Let her have your seat.

ме́ст-ный, local

Ме́стный комите́т про́тив
э́той ме́ры.   The local
committee is against this
measure.

за-ме́ст-и́тель, substitute

Он мой замести́тель.   He is
my substitute.

раз-мещ-а́ть, ⎱ to seat,
раз-мест-и́ть, ⎰ place

Госте́й размести́ли в пе́рвом
ряду́.   The guests were
seated in the first row.

по-ме́щ-ик, landowner

Поме́щик пострада́л от по-
жа́ра. The landowner suf-
fered a loss from the fire.

MET-, SWEEP, TURN

мет-а́ть, } to sweep
мес-ти́,

Служа́нка метёт пол. The
maid sweeps the floor.

мет-ла́, broom

На́до купи́ть но́вую метлу́.
(We) must buy a new broom.

мет-е́ль, blizzard, snowstorm

Из-за́ мете́ли они́ оста́лись
до́ма. They had to stay
home because of a blizzard.

МИЛ-, DEAR, KIND

ми́л-ый, kind, pleasant, nice

Он о́чень ми́лый челове́к.
He is a very nice (pleasant)
man.

ми́л-енький, dear, pretty

Кака́я ми́ленькая де́вочка.
What a pretty little girl!

ми́л-ость, favor, grace, kindness

Ми́лости про́сим! (You are)
welcome!

ми́л-остыня, alms, charity

Ни́щему да́ли ми́лостыню.
They gave alms to the
beggar.

мил-о-се́рдие, mercy, charity

Она́ сестра́ милосе́рдия. She
is a sister of mercy. (She
is a red-cross nurse.)

МИР-, PEACE, WORLD

мир, peace

Вчера́ заключи́ли мир. Peace
was concluded yesterday.

ми́р-ный, peaceful, peace

Ми́рный до́говор подпи́сан.
The peace treaty is signed.

пере-ми́р-ие, truce

Переми́рие продолжа́лось три дня. The truce lasted three days.

по-мир-и́ть, to make peace, reconcile

Их на́до помири́ть. They must be reconciled.

МЛЕК-, МОЛОК-, MILK

млек-о-пита́ющийся, mammal

Коро́ва млекопита́ющееся живо́тное. The cow is a mammal.

млеч-ный, milky

Мле́чный путь я́сно ви́ден на не́бе. The milky way is clearly seen in the sky.

молок-о́, milk

Да́йте мне буты́лку молока́. Give me a bottle of milk.

моло́ч-ник, dairyman, milkman, milk-jug

Моло́чник принёс счёт. The milkman brought the bill.

МЛАД-, МОЛОД-, YOUNG

млад-е́нец, baby, infant, child

Спи мой младе́нец. Sleep, my baby!

млад-е́нчество, infancy, babyhood

Я зна́ю его́ с младе́нчества. I have known him since his infancy.

мла́д-ший, younger

Мла́дший брат в дере́вне. The younger brother is in the country.

молод-ёжь, youth

Золота́я молодёжь прово́дит вре́мя в пра́здности. The gilded youth spend their time in idleness.

молод-е́ть, to grow younger

Вы с ка́ждым днём молоде́ете. You are getting younger every day.

молод-е́ц, brave young fellow, clever fellow

Молодцы́, ребя́та, спаси́бо! You are brave fellows, thank you! (Well done, fellows, thank you!)

молод-о́й, young

Кто э́тот молодо́й челове́к? Who is this young man?

с-мо́лод-у, from the time of one's youth

Он смо́лоду привы́к рабо́тать. He got used to work (he had acquired the habit of working) from the time of his youth.

МН-, МИН-, OPINION

мн-е́ние, opinion, view

Мне хоте́лось бы услы́шать ва́ше мне́ние. I should like to hear your opinion (about it).

мн-и́тельный, mistrustful, suspicious, too anxious about one's health

Моя́ мать о́чень мни́тельна. My mother is too mistrustful. (My mother is too anxious about her health.)

по́-мн-ить, to remember

Не по́мните-ли вы его́ а́дреса? Don't you remember his address?

со-мн-ева́ться, to doubt

Я не сомнева́юсь в его́ че́стности. I don't doubt his honesty.

со-мн-е́ние, doubt

Без сомне́ния вы правы́. Undoubtedly you are right.

вс-по-мин-а́ть, to recall, remember, think of

Мы ча́сто их вспомина́ем. We often think of them.

по-ми́н-ки, a repast in commemoration of a deceased person

Вся семья́ собрала́сь на поми́нки. The whole family came to the memorial repast.

МНОГ-, MANY, MUCH

мно́г-ие, many

Мно́гие из них мне знако́мы. Many of them are familiar to me.

мно́г-о, much, many

Это вы́звало мно́го вопро́сов. This called forth many questions.

мног-о-чи́сленный, numerous

В э́том го́роде многочи́сленное населе́ние. This city has a numerous population.

мно́ж-ество, multitude, lot, great number

У меня́ мно́жество хлопо́т. I have a lot of trouble.

у-множ-а́ть, } to multiply
у-мно́ж-ить, }

Он умно́жил вдво́е свои́ дохо́ды. He doubled his profits.

МОГ-, ABLE, POWER

мог-у́чий, powerful, strong

Он могу́чий боре́ц. He is a powerful wrestler.

моч-ь, to be able

Я ничего́ не могу́ сде́лать. I am unable to do anything.

из-не-мог-а́ть, to be tired, exhausted, to break down

Она́ изнемога́ет от тяжёлого труда́. The heavy work has exhausted her.

по́-мощ-ь, help, assistance

Он нужда́ется в по́мощи. He is in need of help.

мо́ж-но, it is possible, one may, one can

Мо́жно-ли кури́ть? May I (one) smoke?

МОК-, WET

мо́к-нуть, to become wet, soak

Они́ мо́кли под дождём. They were soaking in the rain.

мо́к-рый, wet, damp

Мо́крое полоте́нце виси́т на крючке́. The wet towel is hanging on the hook.

моч-и́ть, to wet, dampen

Он мо́чит го́лову холо́дной водо́й. He wets his head with cold water.

МОЛ-, PRAY

мол-е́бен, Te Deum, thanks-giving service

У́тром служи́ли моле́бен. In the morning they had a Te Deum.

мол-и́тва, prayer

Он зна́ет все моли́твы на-изу́сть. He knows all the prayers by heart.

мол-и́ться, to pray, offer prayers

Стару́шка мо́лится пе́ред ико́ной. The old woman prays before an ikon.

мол-ь-ба́, entreaty, supplica-tion, prayer

Она́ обрати́лась к нему́ с горя́чей мольбо́й. She turned to him with an urgent prayer.

МОЛК-, SILENT, STILL

мо́лк-нуть, to grow still, hush down

Уж по́здно, всё мо́лкнет. It is late, everything is hushed down.

молч-а́ть, to be silent

Почему́ вы всегда́ молчи́те? Why are you always silent?

молч-а́ние, silence

Молча́ние знак согла́сия. Silence gives consent.

в-тихо-мо́лк-у, secretly, silently, noiselessly

Он засмея́лся втихомо́лку. He laughed noiselessly.

МУЖ-, MAN

муж, husband

Муж брани́л жену́. The husband scolded (his) wife.

муж-и́к, peasant

Мужи́к обраба́тывает зе́млю. The peasant cultivates the land.

муж-чи́на, man

В столо́вой бы́ло не́сколько мужчи́н. There were several men in the dining-room.

за́-муж, married, to marry

Она́ неда́вно вы́шла за́муж. She was married recently.

МУК-, FLOUR

мук-а́, flour

Принесли́ мешо́к муки́. They brought a sack of flour.

муч-но́й, farinaceous, flour

От мучно́й пи́щи полне́ют. They get (One gets) stout from (eating) farinaceous food.

мук-о-мо́льня, flour-mill

Мужи́к отвёз зерно́ на муко-мо́льню. The peasant took the grain to the flour-mill.

МУК-, TORTURE, TORMENT

му́к-а, torment, torture

Его́ обрекли́ на ве́чные му́ки. He was doomed to eternal torment.

муч-е́ние, torment, agony, pain, worry, vexation

Муче́ние с ва́ми, да и то́лько. You bring (give) me nothing but worry.

му́ч-ить, to torment, torture

Не му́чьте меня́. Don't torment me!

МУТ-, МЯТ-, TURBID, DISTURB

мут-не́ть, to grow dark, dim, dull

У меня́ в глаза́х мутне́ет. I am fainting. (Everything turns dark before my eyes.)

мýт-ный, turbid, troubled

Он лóвит рыбу в мýтной водé. He is fishing in troubled waters.

мут-ь, muddiness

Это не чай, а какáя-то муть. This is not tea, it's like muddy water.

с-мýт-а, discord, sedition, riot, troubled times

В Россúи смýта. There are troubled times in Russia.

с-мущ-áть, to disturb, perplex, embarrass, confuse

Вы меня смущáете. You embarrass me.

мят-éж, riot

Генерáл усмирúл мятéж. The general has crushed the riot.

без-мят-éжный, quiet, undisturbed, peaceful

Он спал безмятéжным сном. He slept peacefully.

МЫ-, WASH

мы́-ло, soap

Купúте мне кусóк мы́ла. Buy me a cake of soap.

мы-ть, to wash

Онá мóет рýки. She washes her hands.

по-м-óи, slops, dish-water

Помóи вы́плеснули в яму. The slops were splashed into the pit.

МЫСЛ-, THOUGHT

мысл-ь, thought, idea

Это прекрáсная мысль. This is a splendid idea.

мы́сл-ить, to think, reflect, reason

Я мы́слю, слéдовательно, я существýю. I think, therefore I exist.

мысл-úтель, thinker

Егó считáют крýпным мыслúтелем. They consider him a great thinker. (He is considered a great thinker.)

бес-с-мы́сл-ица, nonsense

Это су́щая бессмы́слица. This is sheer nonsense.

вы́-мысел, fiction, invention, fancy

В ска́зке мно́го вы́мысла. There is much fiction in a fairy tale.

вы́-мышл-енный, fictitious

Это не пра́вда, всё э́то вы́мышлено. This is not true, it is all fictitious.

за́-мысел, project, plan, scheme

Никто́ не знал о его́ за́-мыслах. No one knew of his schemes.

про-мы́шл-енник, manufacturer, trader

Промы́шленник уе́хал на я́рмарку. The manufacturer left for the fair.

раз-мышл-е́ние, reflection, pondering, meditation

Он погрузи́лся в глубо́кое размышле́ние. He was lost in thought. (He was absorbed in deep meditation.)

раз-мышл-я́ть, to think, ponder

Мы размышля́ли о значе́нии жи́зни и сме́рти. We were pondering upon the meaning of life and death.

с-мысл, sense, idea, meaning

Како́й смысл э́того расска́за? What is the meaning of this story?

с-мышл-ёный, clever, bright, quick-witted

Он смышлёный па́рень. He is a clever fellow.

Н

НЕГ-, (НѢГ)-, LANGUOR, LUXURY

не́г-а, luxury, languor

Они́ живут в не́ге. They live in luxury.

не́ж-ничать, to pet, caress

По́лно не́жничать, пора́ е́хать! Stop petting, it's time to leave!

нёж-ный, tender, gentle

У неё нёжный гóлос. **She has a gentle voice.**

HEM-, (HѢM)-, NUMB, MUTE

нем-ёть, to get numb

Мой пáльцы немéют от хóлода. **My fingers are getting numb from cold.**

нём-ец, German

Он нéмец рóдом. **He is of German descent.**

нем-éцкий, German

Немéцкий язы́к трýден. **The German language is difficult.**

нем-óй, mute, dumb

Он глух и нем к её прóсьбам. **He is deaf and dumb to her entreaties.**

HEC-, HOC-, CARRY

нес-ти́, to carry, bring

Торгóвка несёт корзи́ну. **The tradeswoman is carrying a basket.**

нос-и́ть, to wear

Я ношý э́ту шýбу вторýю зи́му. **I am wearing this coat the second winter.**

нос-и́лки, stretcher

Рáненого принесли́ на носи́лках. **The wounded man was brought on a stretcher.**

нóш-а, load, burden

Э́та нóша сли́шком тяжелá для вас. **This load is too heavy for you.**

от-нош-éние, attitude, treatment

Меня́ удивля́ет вáше отношéние. **Your attitude amazes me.**

под-нóс, tray

На поднóсе стоя́л графи́н. **A decanter was on the tray.**

с-нóс-ный, passable, tolerable

Их воспи́танник снóсно говори́т по францýзски. **Their pupil (ward) speaks French passably well.**

НЗ-, НОЖ-, KNIFE, PIERCE

во-нз-и́ть, to pierce, plunge	Каза́к вонзи́л кинжа́л по рукоя́ть. The Cossack plunged his dagger to the hilt.
про-нз-и́ть, to pierce	Пу́ля пронзи́ла сте́ну. The bullet pierced the wall.
про-нз-и́тельный, shrill, piercing	Газе́тчик пронзи́тельно за-крича́л. The newspaper man shouted in a shrill voice.
нож, knife	У меня́ нет ножа́. I have no knife.
но́ж-ницы, scissors	Портни́ха ре́жет мате́рию но́жницами. The seam-stress cuts the material (dress goods) with the scissors.

НИЗ-, LOW, BELOW, DOWN

в-низ-у́, down, downstairs	Она́ внизу́. She is down-stairs.
ни́з-кий, low	В э́той ко́мнате ни́зкий пото-ло́к. The ceiling in this room is low.
ни́з-ость, baseness, meanness	Вы спосо́бны на вся́кую ни́зость. You are capable of all kinds of meanness.
ни́ж-ний, lower, under, in-ferior	Ни́жний эта́ж сдаётся. The ground floor is for rent.

НОВ-, NEW

нов-и́нка, news, novelty	Друзья́ собрали́сь посмот-ре́ть на нови́нку. The friends came to have a look at the novelty.

нóв-ый, new

Нам нýжен нóвый учéбник. We need a new textbook.

нóв-шество, innovation

Они́ бы́ли прóтив э́того нóвшества. They were against this innovation.

об-нóв-ка, new purchase, new dress, new thing

Поздравля́ю с обнóвкой. I congratulate you on your purchase.

воз-об-нов-ля́ть, } to renew,
воз-об-нов-и́ть, } resume

Я возобнови́л знакóмство с ним. I have resumed friendly relations with him. (I have resumed my acquaintance with him.)

за́-нов-о, anew, like new

Им пришлóсь отдéлать кварти́ру зáново. They had to redecorate their apartment entirely.

НУД-, NEED

при-нужд-áть,
} to force,
}   compel
при-нуд-и́ть,

Онá принужденá былá согласи́ться. She was forced to agree.

Обстоя́тельства принуди́ли егó продáть дом. The circumstances forced him to sell the house.

нужд-á, need, want

Они́ живýт в нуждé. They live in want.

нужд-áться, to be in need, be in want

Я ни в чём не нуждáюсь. I do not need anything.

нýж-ный, necessary, needed

Он был нýжен отцý. His father needed him.

O

ОБЩ-, COMMON, SOCIAL

общ-е́ственный, social, public

Он дорожи́т обще́ственным мне́нием. He values public opinion.

о́бщ-ество, society

Она́ ре́дко быва́ет в о́бществе. She rarely appears in society.

о́бщ-ий, common, general

У нас о́бщее иму́щество. We have a common property.

общ-е-жи́тие, home, dormitory, asylum

Здесь два общежи́тия для студе́нтов. There are two students homes here.

ОВ-, SHEEP

ов-ца́, sheep

Пасту́х пасёт ове́ц. The shepherd tends his sheep.

ов-е́чий, sheep's

Из ове́чьей ше́рсти ткут мате́рию. They make (weave) dress material of sheep's wool.

ов-чи́нный, sheep's

На нём овчи́нный тулу́п. He wears a sheepskin coat.

ОГН-, ОГОН-, FIRE

ого́н-ь, fire, light

Огни́ уже́ пога́сли. The lights are already out.

огн-ево́й, fire, fiery

Носи́ть огнево́е ору́жие воспреща́ется. It is not allowed to carry firearms.

о́гн-енный, fiery

Со́лнце на́ небе, как о́гненный шар. The sun in the sky is like a fiery sphere (ball).

ОК-, EYE

о́к-о, о́ч-и, } eye	О́ко за о́ко, зуб за́ зуб. An eye for an eye, a tooth for a tooth.
ок-но́, window	Окно́ выхо́дит в сад. The window faces the garden.
оч-ки́, glasses	Где мой очки́? Where are my glasses?
за-о́ч-но, without seeing, out of sight, behind one's back	Я ничего́ не покупа́ю зао́чно. I buy nothing without seeing it first.

П

ПАД-, FALL

пад-а́ть, to fall, drop	Я́блоко па́дает с де́рева. An apple drops from the tree.
па́д-кий, inclined, having a weakness	Он па́док на лесть. He has a weakness for flattery.
про-па́с-ть(про-пад-ть), to disappear, perish	Куда́ вы пропа́ли? Where did you disappear?
у-па́с-ть, to fall	Ма́льчик упа́л с ло́шади. The boy fell down from a horse.
за́-пад, west	Со́лнце кло́нится к за́паду. The sun is rolling westward.
за́-пад-ник, westerner	Турге́нев был за́падником. Turgenev was a westerner.
на-пад-е́ние, attack, assault	Но́чью соверши́ли нападе́ние. The attack was made at night.
при-па́д-ок, fit, attack	Мой дед страда́ет припа́дками. My grandfather suffers from fits.

у-пáд-ок, decline, decay, weakness, collapse, breakdown

У мýжа полнéйший упáдок сил. (Her, my) husband has had a breakdown.

ПАЛ-, ПЛ-, ПЕЛ-, FIRE, FLAME

пал-и́ть, to fire, singe, burn, scorch

Паля́т из пýшек. They are firing the guns.

пал-ь-бá, firing, cannonade

Началáсь уби́йственная пальбá. A deadly cannonade was started.

вос-пал-éние, inflammation

У неё воспалéние лёгких. She is stricken with pneumonia.

за-пáл-ь-чивый, quick-tempered

Он óчень запáльчив. He is a quick-tempered man.

пл-áмя, flame

Вспы́хнуло ослепи́тельное плáмя. A dazzling flame flared up.

пл-áменный, fiery, flaming, ardent

Он уверя́л её в плáменной любви́. He was assuring her of his ardent love.

пé-пел, ashes

От кострá остáлся тóлько пéпел. Only the ashes remained from the bonfire.

пé-пел-ь-ница, ash-tray

На столé нет пéпельницы. There is no ash-tray on the table.

ПАР-, STEAM

пар, steam, vapour, mist

Веснóй пар от земли́ идёт. In spring the mist comes up from the ground.

пáр-ить, to steam, stew

На дворé сегóдня пáрит. The weather is sultry today.

пар-о-вóз, steam-engine, locomotive

Паровóз пыхти́т в гóру. The engine is puffing up-hill.

пар-о-хо́д, steamer, boat

На парохо́де мно́го пасса-
жи́ров. There are many
passengers on board.

ис-пар-я́ться, to evaporate

В жару́ вода́ испаря́ется
бы́стро. In hot weather
water evaporates quickly.

ПАС-, TEND, HERD

пас-ти́, to tend, herd

Он пасёт коро́в. He tends
the cows.

пас-ту́х, shepherd

Пасту́х со ста́дом возвра-
ща́ется в дере́вню. The
shepherd with his flock is
returning to the village.

па́с-т-бище, pasture

На па́стбище мно́го скота́.
In the pasture there are
many cattle.

за-па́с, stock, store, supply,
provision

У нас большо́й запа́с зерна́.
We have a large supply of
grain.

при-па́с-ы, supplies, provisions

Она́ отпра́вилась за с'ест-
ны́ми припа́сами. She
went to get the food sup-
plies (the provisions).

ПАХ-, PLOUGH

па́х-арь, tiller, farmer, ploughman

Па́харь поёт зво́нкую пе́сню.
The ploughman sings a
sonorous song.

пах-а́ть, to plough

Их на́няли паха́ть по́ле.
They were hired to plough
the field.

па́ш-ня, tillage, field

На па́шне зеленеет о́зимь.
The winter corn (grain)
looks green in the field.

ПАХ-, SMELL

пáх-нуть, to smell

Рóза приятно пáхнет. The rose smells pleasant. The rose has a pleasant smell.

пах-ýчий, fragrant

Онá держáла пахýчий цветóк. She held a fragrant flower.

зá-пах, smell, odour, scent

Какóй здесь éдкий зáпах! What an acrid smell is here!

ПЕК-, BAKE

пéк-арь, baker

Пéкарь продаёт хлеб. The baker sells bread.

пек-áрня, bakery

Егó послáли в пекáрню. He was sent to the bakery.

печ-ь (пек-ть), to bake

Когдá вы бýдете печь пирогú? When will you bake the pies?

печ-éнье, baking, pastry, cookies

К чáю пóдали печéнье. The pastry was served at tea.

пéч-ка, stove

Старúк грéется у пéчки. The old man is warming himself at the stove.

пéч-ень, liver

У негó расширéние пéчени. He has a distended liver.

печ-áль, sadness, sorrow

На её лицé печáль. She looks sad. (There is sadness in her face.)

о-пек-ýн, guardian

Мой опекýн чéстный человéк. My guardian is an honest man.

ПЕР-, ПИР-, ПОР-, LOCK, SHUT

за-пир-áть,⎫ to shut,
за-пер-éть,⎭ lock

Я забы́л заперéть дверь. I forgot to shut (lock) the door.

вза-пер-ти́, to be shut up, under lock and key

Она́ сиди́т взаперти́. She is shut in.

о-пир-а́ться, to set, fix, rest, lean

Он опира́лся о стол. He was leaning against the table.

за-по́р, bolt, lock, bar

Э́ти воро́та всегда́ на запо́ре. These gates are always bolted.

у-по́р-ствовать, to persist, resist, to be stubborn

По́лно упо́рствовать, пойдём-те. Enough of your stubbornness, let's go!

ПЕ-, (ПѢ)-, SING

пе-ть, to sing

Вы хорошо́ поёте. You sing well.

пе-ве́ц, singer

О́перный певе́ц вы́шел на сце́ну. An opera singer appeared on the stage.

пе́-ние, singing

Я люблю́ церко́вное пе́ние. I like church singing.

пе́-сня, song

Э́то наро́дная пе́сня. This is a folk song.

пе-ту́х, rooster

Пету́х пропе́л три ра́за. The rooster crowed three times.

на-пе́-в, tune

Мне знако́м э́тот напе́в. This tune is familiar to me.

на-рас-пе́-в, in a singsong voice, to intone

Он чита́л моли́тву нараспе́в. He was reading (saying) the prayer in a singsong voice.

ПЕЧАТ-, (ПЕК)-, SEAL, PRINT

печа́т-ь, seal, print

К письму́ прило́жена печа́ть. A seal is attached to the letter. (The letter is sealed.)

печа́т-ать, to print, publish

Эту ру́копись ско́ро бу́дут печа́тать. This manuscript will soon be printed (published).

рас-печа́т-ывать ⎱ to open, break
рас-печа́т-ать, ⎰ open, unseal

Конто́рщик распеча́тывает паке́т. The clerk is opening the parcel.

в-печат-ле́ние, imprint, impression

Он произвёл на меня́ хоро́шее впечатле́ние. He made a good impression on me.

о-печа́т-ка, misprint

В кни́ге мно́го опеча́ток. There are many misprints in the book.

ПИ-, ПОЙ-, DRINK

пи-ть, to drink

Я хочу́ пить. I want a drink. (I am thirsty.)

пи-тьё, beverage

Что э́то за питьё? What kind of beverage is it?

пь-яне́ть, to get drunk

От э́того вина́ бы́стро пьяне́ют. This wine makes one drunk quickly.

пь-я́ный, drunken man, drunkard

Пья́ный шата́лся по у́лице. The drunken man was staggering on the street.

пи́-во, beer

Не хоти́те-ли пи́ва? Would you like some beer?

пи-вна́я, beer-saloon, barroom

Пойдёмте в пивну́ю. Let's go to the (beer) saloon.

на-пи́-ться, to drink, to slake one's thirst, to get drunk

Они́ напили́сь. They drank enough. (They got drunk.)

за-по́й, fit of hard drinking

Он пьёт запоем. He has fits of hard drinking.

на-пои́-ть, to give to drink

Чем бы вас напои́ть? What shall I offer you to drink?

по-пой-ка, spree, drinking-bout

У студе́нтов была́ попо́йка. The students had a spree.

ПИС-, WRITE

пис-а́ть, to write

Уме́ете-ли вы писа́ть? Can you write?

пис-а́тель, writer, author

Писа́тель напеча́тал но́вый рома́н. The writer has published a new novel.

пис-ь-мо́, letter

Мы ещё не получи́ли ва́шего письма́. We have not received your letter yet.

за-пи́с-ка, note

Оста́вьте ему́ запи́ску. Leave him a note.

о́-пис-ь, list, inventory

Они́ соста́вили о́пись иму́щества. They made an inventory.

пере-пи́с-ка, correspondence

Ме́жду ни́ми завяза́лась перепи́ска. A correspondence started between them.

рас-пис-а́ние, schedule, time-table

Доста́ньте расписа́ние по-ездо́в. Get me a (train) schedule. (Get me a time-table.)

ПИСК-, SQUEAK

писк, squeak, peep, chirp, cheep

В сара́е писк цыпля́т. The chicks peep in the barn.

писк-ли́вый, squeaky

У э́того профе́ссора пискли́вый го́лос. This professor has a squeaky voice.

пищ-а́ть, to squeak, whine, wail

В лю́льке пища́л младе́нец. The infant wailed in the cradle.

ПИТ-, FEED, NOURISH

пит-а́ть, to foster, nourish, feed, cherish	Надéжда юношей питáет. Youth is nourished by hope.
пит-áние, nourishment	Вам необходи́мо уси́ленное питáние. You need a nourishing food. (You need a high caloric diet.)
пи́щ-а, food	Пóвар приготóвил вкýсную пи́щу. The cook has prepared a savory dish.
вос-пи́т-ывать,⎫ to bring up, вос-пит-áть, ⎭ educate	Они́ хорошó воспи́тывают своегó сы́на. They are bringing up their son well.

ПЛАТ-, ПОЛОТ-, DRESS, LINEN

плáт-ье, dress	На ней нóвое плáтье. She is wearing a new dress.
плат-óк, handkerchief	В кармáне носовóй платóк. A handkerchief is in the pocket.
плащ, cloak, wrap	Он купи́л непромокáемый плащ. He bought a waterproof cloak.
полот-éнце, towel	Принеси́те чи́стое полотéнце. Bring me a clean towel.
полот-нó, linen	Бáба соткалá кусóк полотнá. The peasant woman has woven a piece of linen.
полот-ня́ный, linen	На постéли полотня́ная простыня́. A linen sheet is on the bed.

ПЛАТ-, PAY

плáт-а, pay, payment, fee, charge, salary, wages	Онá получáет ни́зкую плáту за труд. She gets low wages for her work.

плат-ёж, payment

Наступи́л срок платежа́. Payday has come.

плат-и́ть, to pay

За кварти́ру я плачу́ вперёд. I pay in advance for my apartment. (I pay my rent in advance.)

бес-пла́т-ный, free of charge

Они́ у́чатся в беспла́тной шко́ле. They attend (study in) a free school.

ПЛЕТ-, WEAVE

плѐт-ень, fence, wattle

Наш плѐтень сде́лан из пру́тьев. Our fence is made of wattle rods.

плет-ь, lash, whip

Он бил ло́щадь плѐтью. He was lashing his horse.

плес-ти́, to weave, tat

Крестья́нки плету́т то́нкое кру́жево. The peasant women weave fine lace.

за-плет-а́ть, to braid, plait

Де́вушка заплета́ет ко́су. The young girl braids her hair.

пере-плес-ти́, to bind, interlace

Мне на́до переплести́ э́тот слова́рь. I must have a binding for this dictionary.

пере-плёт, cover, binding

Сде́лайте ко́жаный переплёт. Make a leather binding.

ПЛОСК-, FLAT

пло́ск-ий, flat, trivial

Э́то пло́ская шу́тка. This is a trivial joke.

пло́ск-ость, flat, plane

Мы стои́м на ро́вной пло́скости. We are on a level plane.

площ-áдка, platform, landing, patio

Пéред дóмом площáдка. There is a patio in front of the house.

плóщ-адь, square, esplanade

На плóщади мнóго нарóду. There are many people in the square.

ПЛЫ-, ПЛАВ-, SWIM, FLOAT

плы-ть, to swim, float

Трýдно плыть прóтив течéния. It is difficult to go (swim) against the tide.

от-плы́т-ие, departure, sailing

Отплы́тие парохóда в два часá. The boat sails at two o'clock.

плáв-ать, to swim

Я учýсь плáвать. I am learning to swim.

плáв-ание, trip, voyage, navigation

Моря́к отправился в плáвание. The seaman went off to sea.

ПОЛК-, REGIMENT

полк, regiment

В гóроде стоит полк. There is a regiment in town.

полк-óвник, colonel

Наш полкóвник строг. Our colonel is strict.

полк-овóй, regimental

На балý игрáл полковóй оркéстр. The regimental band played at the ball.

о-полч-éние, militia

Начáльник ополчéния дал прикáз выступáть. The head of the militia gave orders to start.

о-полч-и́ться, to take arms, rise against

Вся рать ополчи́лась прóтив негó. The entire host rose against him.

ПОЛН-, FULL

полн-е́ть, to become stout

Вы сли́шком полне́ете. You are getting too stout.

по́лн-ый, full

У них по́лон дом госте́й. Their house is full of guests.

вы-полн-я́ть,⎫ to carry out,
вы́-полн-ить,⎭ execute, fulfil

Они́ вы́полнили зада́ние. They have carried out the task.

ис-полн-е́ние, fulfilment, execution

Прика́з приведён в исполне́ние. The order (verdict) was carried out.

по-по́лн-ить, to fill up, supplement, add

Он хо́чет попо́лнить пробе́лы своего́ образова́ния. He wants to fill the gaps in his education.

ПРАВ-, TRUTH, RIGHT

пра́в-да, truth

Он не всегда́ говори́т пра́вду. He does not always speak the truth.

пра́в-ило, rule, principle

Нет пра́вила без исключе́ния. There is no rule without an exception.

пра́в-ить, to rule

Дикта́тор пра́вит желе́зной руко́й. The dictator rules (governs) with an iron hand.

пра́в-ый, right, correct

Вы, как всегда́, правы́. As usual, you are right.

прав-о-сла́вный, orthodox

Она́ правосла́вного вероиспове́дания. She is of orthodox faith.

ПРАХ-, ПОРОХ-, DUST, POWDER

прах, dust, earth, ruin

Всё пошло́ пра́хом. All went to rack and ruin.

по́рох, gun powder	На скла́де взорва́лся по́рох. The gun powder exploded in the warehouse.
порох-ово́й, gun powder	На порохово́м заво́де забасто́вка. There is a strike at the gunpowder works.
порош-о́к, powder	Мне ну́жен зубно́й порошо́к. I need some tooth powder.

ПРЕТ-, FORBID, ARGUE

за-прещ-а́ть, за-прет-и́ть, } to forbid	Ему́ запреща́ют туда́ ходи́ть. They forbid him to go there.
за-прещ-е́ние, prohibition	Не взира́я на запреще́ние, он вошёл. In spite of the prohibition, he went in.

ПРОС-, BEG

прос-и́ть, to beg, ask, request	Про́сят не шуме́ть. They ask not to make noise.
про́с-ь-ба, request, petition	У меня́ к вам больша́я про́сьба. I have a great favor to ask of you.
прош-е́ние, application	Проше́ние уже́ по́дано. The application has already been presented.
до-про́с, examination, inquest, hearing	Его́ повели́ на допро́с. He was taken to an inquest.
с-прос, demand	На э́тот това́р нет спро́су. There is no demand for this merchandise.

ПРОСТ-, SIMPLE, EXCUSE

прост-о́й; simple	Э́то о́чень просто́й приме́р. This is a very simple example.

прост-отá, simplicity, frankness, artlessness

Егó уважáют за простотý обращéния. They respect him for his artless manners.

прощ-áть, } to forgive
прост-и́ть, }

Прости́те меня́ пожáлуйста. Please forgive me.

прощ-éние, forgiveness, pardon, excuse

Он заслýживает прощéния. He deserves forgiveness (pardon).

ПРУГ-, ПРЯГ-, SPRING, HARNESS

у-прýг-ий, elastic, resilient, springy

У негó упрýгие мýскулы. He has an elastic body (muscles).

пруж-и́на, spring

В часáх сломáлась пружи́на. The watch spring broke.

су-прýг-а, wife

Приходи́те к нам с супрýгой. Come and see us with your wife.

су-прýж-еский, wedded

Супрýжеская жизнь егó привлекáла. Wedded life appealed to him.

в-пряг-áть, to harness

В телéгу впрягáют пáру волóв. A yoke of oxen is harnessed to a cart.

на-пряж-éние, strain, stress, effort

Эта рабóта трéбует огрóмного напряжéния. This work takes an awful lot of effort. (This work is very strenuous.)

ПРЫГ-, JUMP

пры́г-ать, } to jump
пры́г-нуть, }

Ктó-то пры́гнул чéрез забóр. Someone jumped over the fence.

прыж-óк, jump, leap, somersault

Он сдéлал большóй прыжóк. He turned a somersault.

ПРЯД-, STRAND, YARN, SPIN

пряд-ь, strand, twist, yarn, lock, tuft

Она́ отре́зала прядь воло́с. She cut off a strand of hair.

пряд-и́льный, spinning

Рабо́тница поступи́ла на прядѝльную фа́брику. The factory woman went to work at a spinning mill.

пряс-ть, to spin

Вам сле́дует научи́ться прясть. You must learn to spin.

пря́ж-а, yarn, thread

Стару́ха несёт пря́жу домо́й. The old woman takes the yarn home.

пря́х-а, spinner

Пря́ха сиди́т за веретено́м. The spinner is sitting at the spinning-wheel.

ПТ-, BIRD

пт-и́ца, bird

Пти́ца вьёт гнездо́. The bird is building a nest.

пт-ене́ц, fledgeling

На траве́ пищи́т птене́ц. The fledgeling is chirping in the grass.

пт-а́шка, little bird

Пта́шка клюёт зерно́. The little bird is pecking the grain.

ПУГ-, FRIGHT

пуг-а́ть, to frighten, startle

Не пуга́йте её. Don't frighten her.

пуг-ли́вый, timid, shy, fearful

На́ша ло́шадь пугли́ва. Our horse shies.

ис-пу́г, fear, fright

Она́ побледне́ла от испу́га. She turned pale with fright.

ПУСК-, ПУСТ-, LET

пуск-а́ть, }
пуст-и́ть, } to let, allow, permit

Его́ не пуска́ют к реке́. They won't let him go to the river.

Пусть он де́лает как хо́чет. Let him do as he pleases.

вы-пуск-но́й, final

Она́ провали́лась на вы-пускно́м экза́мене. She failed at the final examination.

о́т-пуск, leave of absence

Он уе́хал в о́тпуск. He went away on a leave.

про́-пуск, pass, permit

Мне да́ли про́пуск. They gave me a pass.

у-пущ-е́ние, omission, negligence, fault, mistake, oversight

Это упуще́ние тру́дно испра́вить. It is difficult to correct this mistake.

ПУСТ-, EMPTY

пуст-о́й, empty, vacant, futile, idle, frivolous

Они́ веду́т пусто́й о́браз жи́зни. They lead an empty life.

пуст-ы́ня, desert

В пусты́нях обыкнове́нно живу́т коче́вники. The nomads usually live in the deserts.

пуст-ы́рь, vacant lot

Этот пусты́рь преврати́ли в парк. This vacant lot was turned into a park.

пуст-я́к, trifle, nothing, nonsense

Всё э́то пустяки́! All this is a mere trifle.

пуст-я́чный, trivial, trifling, paltry, petty

Это пустя́чное предприя́тие. This is a trivial project.

ПУТ-, ROAD, WAY

пут-ь, road, way, trip, journey

Счастли́вого пути́!   Happy
journey!

пут-ево́й, travelling

Его́ путевы́е заме́тки поя-
ви́лись в печа́ти. His travelling notes appeared in
print.

по-пу́т-чик, fellow-traveller

Я вам не попу́тчик. I am
not your fellow-traveller.

ПУХ-, DOWN

пух, down

Из поду́шки вы́сыпался пух.
The down came out of the
pillow.

пух-ово́й, down, downy

У неё пухово́е одея́ло. She
has a downy comforter.

пуш-и́стый, downy, fluffy

Она́ заку́талась в пуши́стый
плато́к. She muffled herself in a fluffy shawl.

пу́х-нуть, to swell

Щека́ ста́ла пу́хнуть. The
cheek began to swell.

о́-пух-оль, swelling, tumour

На ноге́ появи́лась о́пухоль.
There appeared a swelling
on the leg.

пу́х-лый, plump, chubby

Ко мне тя́нутся пу́хлые
ру́чки. Chubby little hands
stretch out towards me.

ПЫТ-, TRY, ATTEMPT

пыт-а́ться, to attempt, try

Я пыта́лась не́сколько раз
зайти́ к вам.   I made
several attempts to call on
you.

до-пы́т-ываться, to poke and
pry, question, try to find
out

Чего́ вы всё вре́мя допы́ты-
ваетесь? What are you
trying to find out?

ó-пыт, experiment, test	В лаборатóрии производи́ли óпыт. An experiment was being made in the laboratory.
по-пы́т-ка, attempt	Он сдéлал попы́тку к бéгству. He made an attempt to escape.
пы́т-ка, torture, torment	Его́ подвéргли морáльной пы́тке. He was subjected to mental torture.

Р
РАБ-, SLAVE

раб, slave	Он раб своéй стрáсти. He is a slave of his passion.
рáб-ство, slavery	Человéчество освободи́лось от рáбства. Mankind has freed itself from slavery.
раб-óта, work	У меня́ мнóго рабóты. I have much work to do.
раб-óтать, to work	Они́ рабóтают по цéлым дням. They work all day long.
раб-óчий, workman	Рабóчие бастýют. The workmen are on strike.

РАВ-, EQUALITY

рáв-енство, equality	Рáвенство тóлько мечтá. Equality is only a dream.
рав-ни́на, plain	Пéред нáми однообрáзная равни́на. A monotonous plain is before us.
рáв-ный, equal, match, like, similar	Емý нет рáвного. There is no one like him.

с-рав-нéние, comparison

Не дéлайте такúх сравнéний. Don't make such comparisons.

РАД-, GLAD

рáд-ость, joy, gladness

Онá прыгает от рáдости. She is dancing for joy.

рáд-остный, glad, joyous, cheerful

Мы получúли рáдостное извéстие. We received the glad tidings.

рад-ýшный, cordial, affable, hospitable

Егó прúняли радýшно. They met him hospitably. (They met him cordially.)

РАЗ-, ONCE, FELL, DEFEAT, IMPRINT, INFLICT

раз, once

Я был там тóлько раз. I was there only once.

раз-úть, to fell, strike

Слóво сильнéе пýли разúт. The word strikes more powerfully than a bullet.

воз-раж-áть, to object, retort, contradict

Вам нéчего возражáть на áто. You have nothing to say to this. (You cannot object to this.)

за-рáз-а, contagion, infection

Зарáза быстро распространúлась. The contagion spread fast.

óб-раз, image, shape, form, manner, trend

Мне не нрáвится ваш óбраз мыслей. I don't like the trend of your thoughts.

об-рáз-чик, sample

Дáйте ей обрáзчик áтой матéрии. Give her a sample of this material.

без-об-рáз-ие, deformity, unseemliness, indecency, disorder

Что за безобрáзие! How indecent! (What a shame!)

РАЗ-, DIFFERENT

рáз-ница, difference
Рáзница в ценé небольшáя. There is a small difference in price.

рáз-ный, different
У нас рáзные вкýсы. We have different tastes.

раз-но-об-рáз-ный, diverse, various
Ученикú писáли на разнообрáзные тéмы. The pupils wrote on various topics.

РЕЗ-, (РѢЗ)-, CUT

рéз-ать, to cut
Хозя́йка рéжет хлеб. The hostess cuts the bread.

рéз-кий, sharp, cutting, harsh
Письмó напúсано рéзко. The letter is written harshly.

рез-ня́, massacre, butchery
Рáспря кóнчилась резнёй. The feud ended in a massacre.

от-рéз-ать, to cut
Отрéжьте мне кусóк сы́ру. Cut a slice of cheese for me.

РЕШ-, (РѢШ)-, DECIDE, SOLVE

реш-áть,⎫ to work out, solve, decide
реш-úть,⎭
реш-éние, decision
Онú решúли задáчу. They worked out the problem.
К какóму решéнию вы пришлú? To what decision have you come?

реш-úтельный, resolute, determined, bold
Это решúтельный постýпок. This is a resolute (bold) action.

раз-реш-éние, permission, permit, license
Емý вы́дали разрешéние на вы́езд. They gave him a permit to go abroad.

РОД-, BIRTH, TRIBE, NATURE

род, family, generation, tribe, native
Он рóдом из Москвы́. He is a native of Moscow.

рóд-ина, native country
Онá уéхала на рóдину. She went to her native country.

| род-и́ть, | } to give birth | Жена́ родила́ ему́ сы́на. **The** wife bore him a son. (His wife gave birth to a son.) |
| рож-а́ть, | | |

род-и́тели, parents — Мои́ роди́тели о́чень стары́. My parents are very old.

род-но́й, kin, own — Он мой родно́й брат. He is my own brother.

на-ро́д, people — Ру́сский наро́д гостеприи́-мен. The Russian people are hospitable.

при-ро́д-а, nature, structure — Я изуча́ю приро́ду расте́ний. I am studying the nature (structure) of plants.

у-ро́д, monster, ugly being — Посмотри́те на э́того уро́да. Look at this monster.

у-рож-а́й, harvest — В э́том году́ хоро́ший уро-жа́й. The harvest is good this year.

рожд-е́ние, birth — Поздравля́ю с днём рожде́-ния. I congratulate (you) upon your birthday.

воз-рожд-е́ние, regeneration, renascence, renaissance — Эпо́ха возрожде́ния. The period of renaissance.

РОСТ-, РАСТ-, GROWTH

рост, stature — Челове́к высо́кого ро́ста. A tall man (of tall stature).

| раст-и́, | } to grow | В по́ле растёт трава́. The grass grows in the field. |
| рост-и́, | | |

ро́с-лый (рост-лый), tall — В э́том полку́ ро́слые сол-да́ты. There are tall sol-diers in this regiment.

раст-е́ние, plant — У нас мно́го ре́дких расте́ний. We have many rare plants.

вóз-раст, age

Мы одногó вóзраста с ним. We are of the same age as he.

рóщ-а, grove

Недалекó отсю́да берёзовая рóща. There is a grove of birches not far from here.

РУБ-, CUT, CHOP, LIMIT

руб-и́ть, to cut, chop

Он рýбит дровá.   He is chopping wood.

руб-éж, border, limit

Мой дя́дя живёт за рубежóм. My uncle lives beyond the border.   (My uncle lives abroad.)

рýб-ленный, cut, chopped

Они́ заказáли рýбленные котлéты.   They ordered some (minced) meat balls.

руб-ль, rouble

Одолжи́те мне рубль. Lend me a rouble.

РУК-, HAND, VOUCH

рук-á, hand, arm

Он замахáл рукáми.   He began to wave his hands.

рук-áв, sleeve

Рукáв пóрван. The sleeve is torn.

рук-ави́ца, mitten

Возьми́те с собóй рукави́цы. Take your mittens.

руч-áться, to vouch, guarantee

Я за негó ручáюсь.   I vouch for him.

по-рýк-а, surety, pledge, bail

Егó отпусти́ли на порýки. He was released on bail.

по-руч-éние, errand, commission

Не давáйте ей поручéний. Don't give her any errands.

РЫБ-, FISH

рыб-а, fish

В э́том о́зере мно́го ры́бы. There are plenty of fish in this lake.

рыб-а́к, fisherman

Вот идёт рыба́к с у́дочкой. There goes the fisherman with his rod.

рыб-а́чий, fisherman's, fishing

Волна́ опроки́нула рыба́чью ло́дку. The wave overturned the fishing smack.

рыб-оло́вство, fishing

Рыболо́вство вы́годный про́мысел. Fishing is a profitable trade.

С

САД-, СЕД-, (СѢД)-, СИД-, SIT, SEAT

сад, garden

Мы гуля́ем в саду́. We walk in the garden.

сад-и́ться, to sit down, be seated

Сади́тесь пожа́луйста. Please sit down. (Please be seated.)

сад-о́вник, gardener

Садо́вник продаёт цветы́. The gardener sells flowers.

саж-а́ть, to plant

Он сажа́ет дере́вья. He is planting trees.

у-сад-ь-ба, homestead, country seat

Пе́ред на́ми уса́дьба. Before us there is a country seat.

у-са́ж-иваться, to be seated, take one's seat

Уса́живайтесь, господа́! Be seated, gentlemen! (Take your seats, gentlemen!)

сес-ть (сѣд-ть), to sit, get into, get at

Пора́ сесть за рабо́ту. It's time to start (get at) the work.

сед-ло́, saddle

Он е́здит верхо́м без седла́. He rides on horseback without a saddle.

за-сед-а́ние, conference, meeting	Сего́дня не бу́дет заседа́ния. There will be no conference today.
пред-сед-а́тель, chairman	Председа́тель за́нял ме́сто. The chairman took his seat.
сид-е́ть, ⎫ to sit,	Он сиди́т в кре́сле. He is sitting in an arm-chair.
по-сид-е́ть, ⎭ to sit, stay	Посиди́те ещё не́сколько мину́т. Stay a few minutes longer.

<u>СВЕТ-</u>, (СВѢТ)-, LIGHT, WORLD

свет, light, world	Он об'е́здил весь свет. He has travelled all over the world.
свет-а́ть, to grow light	Уже́ света́ет. It is getting light. (It is already dawn.)
свет-ле́ть, to clear up, get brighter	Не́бо светле́ет. The sky is clearing.
све́т-лый, bright, light-colored	На ней све́тлое пла́тье. She is wearing a light-colored dress.
све́т-ский, worldly, mundane, secular	Его́ счита́ют све́тским челове́ком. He is considered a worldly man. (He is considered a man of the world.)
свеч-а́, candle	Свеча́ догора́ет. The candle is burning low.
про-све́ч-ивать, to shine through, to be translucent, pass through	Со́лнце просве́чивает сквозь облака́. The sun shines through the clouds.
про-свещ-е́ние, enlightenment, education	Он выступа́ет про́тив наро́дного просвеще́ния. He comes out against popular education.

СВОБ-, FREE

своб-о́да, freedom, liberty

Я даю́ вам по́лную свобо́ду де́йствия. I am giving you complete freedom of action. (I am giving you a free hand.)

о-своб-оди́ть, to free, release

Его́ не ско́ро освободя́т. They won't release him soon.

о-своб-ожда́ться, to get free, get off

В кото́ром часу́ вы освобожда́етесь? At what time do you get off?

СВЯТ-, HOLY

свят-и́ть, to sanctify, consecrate, bless

Вчера́ святи́ли но́вые знамёна. Yesterday they consecrated the new banners.

свят-о́й, saint, saintly, holy

Свята́я Русь — на́ша ро́дина. Holy Russia is our mother country.

свят-ки, yuletide, Christmas holidays

На свя́тках мно́го весёлых игр. At Christmas time there are many merry games.

свящ-е́нник, priest

Свяще́нник вы́нес распя́тие. The priest brought out the crucifix.

СЕ-, (СѢ)-, SEED, SOW

се́-ять, to sow

Крестья́не се́ют пшени́цу. The peasants are sowing the wheat.

се́-мя, seed, grain

Се́мя упа́ло на хоро́шую по́чву. The grain fell on fertile ground.

се-ть, net, network

Егó лицó покрыто сéтью морщúн. His face is covered with a network of wrinkles.

сé-тка, net

Бáбочка попáла в сéтку. The butterfly got into a net. (The butterfly was caught in a net.)

СЕК-, (СѢК)-, AXE, CHOP

сек-úра, axe, hatchet, battle-axe

Сéкира старúнное орýжие. The battle-axe is an ancient weapon.

сеч-ь, to whip, flog, thrash

Егó чáсто секлú. He was often flogged.

на-сек-óмое, insect

В огорóде мнóго насекóмых. There are many insects in the vegetable garden.

пере-сек-áть, to cross, cut into, intersect

Оврáг пересекáет дорóгу. The ravine cuts into the road.

СЕРД-, СЕРЕД-, СРЕД-, HEART, MIDDLE, MEAN

сéрд-це, heart

У негó слáбое сéрдце. He has a weak heart.

серд-éчный, hearty, cordial

Шлю вам сердéчный привéт. I am sending you my cordial greetings.

серд-úться, to be angry, to fret

Не сердúтесь на меня. Don't be angry with me!

серед-úна, middle

Мы éдем на дáчу в середúне лéта. In the middle of summer we are going to the country.

сред-á, environment, surroundings, medium

Средá егó загубúла. The environment ruined him.

срéд-ний, middle

Человéк срéдних лет. A middle-aged man.

срéд-ство, means

У них ограни́ченные срéдства. Their means are limited.

по-срéд-ник, intermediary, agent

Он посрéдник по продáже недви́жимости. He is a real-estate agent.

СКАК-, LEAP

скак-áть, to leap, bound, gallop

Кто скáчет на конé? Who is galloping there?

скач-óк, jump, leap, skip

Он сдéлал большóй скачóк. He made one big leap.

скáч-ки, horse-race

Мы бы́ли на скáчках. We were at the horse-race.

вы́-скоч-ка, upstart

Я не люблю́ вы́скочек. I don't like upstarts.

СЛ-, СОЛ-, СЫЛ-, SEND

сл-ать, to send

Он шлёт письмó по воздýшной пóчте. He is sending a letter by air mail.

при-сл-áть, to send

Нам прислáли билéты на концéрт. They sent us concert tickets.

по-сóл, ambassador

Рýсский посóл при́был в Вашингтóн. The Russian ambassador arrived in Washington.

по-сóл-ь-ство, embassy

Мой брат слýжит в посóльстве. My brother is employed at the embassy.

по-сыл-áть, to send

Онá посылáет нам цветы́ кáждый день. She sends us flowers every day.

по-сы́л-ка, parcel, package

Получи́ли-ли вы посы́лку? Did you receive the package?

с-сы́л-ь-ный, convict, exile

Оди́н из ссы́льных бежа́л. One of the convicts escaped.

СЛАВ-, СЛОВ-, СЛУ-, СЛЫ-, SLAV, FAME, WORD, KNOW, HEAR

сла́в-а, fame, glory, renown

Сла́ва Бо́гу, она́ вы́здоровела. Thank God (Glory to God), she has recovered!

сла́в-иться, to have a reputation, to be famous

Э́тот край сла́вится свои́м кли́матом. This country is famous for its climate.

сла́в-ный, famous, renowned, nice

Ваш оте́ц сла́вный челове́к. Your father is a nice man.

слав-яни́н, Slav

Среди́ славя́н мно́го музыка́нтов. There are many musicians among the Slavs.

слав-я́нский, Slavic

Мы изуча́ем славя́нские языки́. We are studying Slavic languages.

сло́в-о, word

За ва́ми после́днее сло́во. You have the last word.

слов-а́рь, dictionary

Мне ну́жен ру́сско-англи́йский слова́рь. I need a Russian-English dictionary.

преди-сло́в-ие, preface

Я уже́ написа́л предисло́вие. I have already written the preface.

со-сло́в-ие, estate, social class

Вы како́го сосло́вия? To what social class do you belong? (What is your social status?)

благо-слов-ля́ть, to bless, to give one's blessings

Благослови́те меня́, ба́тюшка! Bless me, father!

слу-х, rumour, report, hearing, ear, news, talk

Хо́дят слу́хи о госуда́рственном переворо́те. There are rumours about the overthrow of the government.

в-слу-х, aloud

Чита́йте всегда́ вслух. Always read aloud.

слу́-шать, to hear, listen, heed

Я слу́шаю вас со внима́нием. I always pay attention to what you say. (I always heed you.)

по-слу-шный, obedient

Он послу́шный ма́льчик. He is an obedient boy.

слы-ть, to be reputed, to be considered

У нас он слывёт у́мником. Among us he has a reputation for being clever.

слы́-шать, to hear

Я сама́ слы́шала э́то. I heard this myself.

СЛАД-, SWEET

слад-кий, sweet, dessert

Мать гото́вит сла́дкое блю́до. The mother is making a dessert.

слас-ти, sweets, sweetmeats

Де́вочка лю́бит сла́сти. The little girl likes sweets.

на-слажд-е́ние, pleasure, delight, enjoyment

Я получи́л большо́е наслажде́ние от ва́шего пе́ния. Your singing gave me great pleasure.

СЛЕД-, (СЛѢД)-, TRACK, TRAIL, FOLLOW, INHERIT

след, trail, track

Наконе́ц мы напа́ли на след. At last we found the track.

след-и́ть, to watch, follow

Я слежу́ за полити́ческими собы́тиями. I follow political events.

слѣ́д-ователь, examining mag-
istrate, coroner, examining
judge

Дѣ́ло пе́редано слѣ́дователю.
The case was handed over
to the examining judge.

на-слѣ́д-ник, heir

Наслѣ́днику оста́вили боль-
шо́е состоя́ние. They left
a large estate to the heir.

по-слѣ́д-ствие, consequence,
result

Ду́мали-ли вы о послѣ́д-
ствиях? Have you thought
of the consequences?

СЛУГ-, SERVE

слуг-а́, servant

Слуга́ отвори́л дверь. The
servant opened the door.

служ-а́нка, maid

Служа́нка принесла́ газе́ты.
The maid brought the newspapers.

слу́ж-ба, employment, work

Я иду́ на слу́жбу. I am
going to work.

служ-и́ть, to work, to be
employed

Он слу́жит в конто́ре. He is
employed at the office.

за-слу́г-а, merit

Она́ получи́ла по заслу́гам.
She got what she deserved.
(She received according to
her merits.)

СМЕ-, (СМѢ)-, LAUGH

сме-х, laughter, laugh

Смех сквозь слёзы. Laughter
through tears.

сме-я́ться, to laugh

Переста́ньте смея́ться. Stop
laughing!

сме-ши́ть, to make one laugh

Вы всегда́ смеши́те меня́.
You always make me laugh.

на-смѣ́-шка, ridicule, mockery

Это не статья́, а про́сто
насмѣ́шка. This is not an
article, it is a sheer mockery.

COX-, CYX-, CЫX-, DRY

сóх-нуть, to dry, get dry, parch | От лихорáдки сóхнут гýбы. The lips are parched with fever.

сух-óй, dry, clear | Стоя́ла сухáя óсень. We had a dry autumn.

сýш-a, land | С корабля́ уви́дели сýшу. The land was seen from the boat.

суш-и́ть, to dry | Онá сýшит вóлосы. She is drying her hair.

вы-сых-áть, to get dry | Лéтом нáше болóто высыхáет. In summer our marsh dries up.

CП-, COH-, CH-, SLEEP

сп-ать, to sleep, take a nap | Спи́те-ли вы днём? Do you sleep (take a nap) in the day-time?

сп-áльня, bedroom | В спáльне две кровáти. There are two beds in the bedroom.

сон, sleep, dream | Меня́ клóнит ко снý. I am sleepy.

сóн-ный, sleepy | Кругóм бы́ло сóнное цáрство. A sleepy kingdom was round about.

бес-сóн-ница, insomnia | Я страдáю бессóнницей. I suffer from insomnia.

за-сн-ýть, to fall asleep | Несмотря́ на шум дéти заснýли. In spite of the noise the children fell asleep.

сн-и́ться, to dream | Мне сни́лся чýдный сон. I had a wonderful dream.

СПЕХ-, (СПѢХ)-, HURRY, SPEED

спех, hurry, haste

Это дело не к спеху. There is no hurry.

спеш-и́ть, to be in a hurry, to rush

Куда́ вы спеши́те? Where are you rushing to?

у-спе́х, success

Ле́кция прошла́ с успе́хом. The lecture was successful.

до-спе́х-и, armour, belongings

Он забра́л свои́ доспе́хи. He took all his belongings.

СТА-, СТОЙ-, СТОЯ-, STAND, BECOME

ста-ть, to become, begin, start

Он стал пить. He started to drink. He began to drink. (He took to drinking.)

в-ста-ва́ть,
в-ста-ть, }to get up

Я встаю́ в шесть часо́в утра́. I get up at six o'clock in the morning.

вы́-ста-вка, exhibit

Эта карти́на ку́плена на вы́ставке. This picture was bought at an exhibit.

за-ста́-ва, gate, barrier

На окра́ине деревя́нная застава. There is a wooden gate on the outskirts (of the town).

на-ста́-вник, tutor

Де́тям необходи́м наста́вник. The children need a tutor.

недо-ста́-ток, fault, shortcoming

У него́ мно́го недоста́тков. He has many shortcomings.

при́-ста-нь, landing, wharf, pier

Паро́ход стои́т у при́стани. The steamer is at the pier.

ста-но́к, lathe

Он рабо́тает на тока́рном станке́. He works on a turning-lathe.

ста-нови́ться, to become

Стано́вится темно́. It is becoming (getting) dark.

со-ста́-в, composition, personnel, body, staff

Министе́рство бы́ло в по́лном соста́ве. The ministry was present in a body.

пред-ста-вле́ние, idea, notion, performance, presentation

Я не име́л представле́ния об э́том. I had no idea about it.

сто́и-ть, to cost, to be worth

Ско́лько сто́ит э́та шля́па? How much is this hat?

сто́й-ка, counter, bar

Прика́зчик стоя́л за сто́йкой. The salesman stood at the counter.

сто́й-кий, sturdy, firm, persevering

У него́ сто́йкий хара́ктер. His is a firm character.

стоя́-ть, to stand, stay

Все стоя́ли как вко́панные. They all stood as if rooted to the spot.

на-стоя́-щий, real

Э́то настоя́щий же́мчуг. This is a real pearl.

со-стоя́-ние, fortune, means, condition

У неё большо́е состоя́ние. She has a great fortune.

СТЕРЕГ-, СТОРОЖ-, СТРОГ-, WATCH, STERN

стере́ч-ь (стерег-ть), to watch, guard, take care

Де́ти стерегу́т лошаде́й. The children are watching the horses.

о-стерег-а́ться, to beware, to be on guard

Остерега́йтесь карма́нщиков. Beware of the pickpockets.

сто́рож, watchman

Сто́рож стои́т у воро́т. The watchman is standing at the gate.

сторож-и́ть, to watch, guard

Соба́ка сторожи́т дом. The dog is guarding (watching) the house.

стро́г-ий, stern, strict

Мой дя́дя о́чень строг. My uncle is very strict.

о-стро́г, prison

Он просиде́л в остро́ге два го́да. He was in the prison two years.

о-сторо́ж-ныи, cautious, careful

Осторо́жней, а то споткнё-тесь! Careful, or you will stumble!

СТРАД-, SUFFER

страд-а́ть, to suffer

Я страда́ю зубно́й бо́лью. I have (suffer from) a toothache.

страд-а́ние, suffering, pain, distress

Её сын причини́л ей мно́го страда́ний. Her son caused her much suffering.

со-страд-а́ние, compassion, pity, sympathy

Э́то несча́стье вы́звало все-о́бщее сострада́ние. This misfortune roused general sympathy.

страс-ть, passion

Страсть ослепля́ет люде́й. Passion blinds people.

при-стра́с-тие, bias, prejudice

Отве́чу вам без пристра́стия. I shall answer you without a bias.

СТРАХ-, FEAR

страх, fear, fright

От стра́ха у меня́ сжа́лось се́рдце. My heart shuddered from fright.

за-страх-ова́ть, to insure

Они́ застрахова́ли своё иму́-щество. They insured their property.

стра́ш-ный, frightful, terrible

Разрази́лся стра́шный уда́р гро́ма. There was a terrible crash of thunder.

СТРЕМ-, BOUND FOR, ASPIRE

стрем-и́ться, to aspire, long, crave

К чему́ вы стреми́тесь? To what are you aspiring?

стрем-ле́ние, aspiration, inclination, tendency

У него́ дурны́е стремле́ния. He has bad inclinations.

стре́м-я, stirrup

Стре́мя оторва́лось. The stirrup is torn off.

стрем-гла́в, headlong

Она́ бро́силась стремгла́в к две́ри. She rushed headlong to the door.

у-стрем-ля́ть,⎫ to direct, turn,
у-стрем-и́ть, ⎭   fix

Он устреми́л свой взор на мо́ре. He turned his gaze to the sea.

СТУД-, СТЫД-, CHILL, SHAME

студ-ёный, chill, cold

В коло́дце студёная вода́. The water is cold in the well.

про-сту́д-а, chill, cold

У меня́ си́льная просту́да. I have a bad cold.

сту́ж-а, cold, frost

На дворе́ сту́жа. It is cold (frost) out.

стыд, shame, disgrace

Это про́сто стыд и срам! (For shame.) This is simply a disgrace!

стыд-и́ться, to be ashamed

Он стыди́лся показа́ться на глаза́. He was ashamed to come.

сты́-нуть (стыд-нуть), to grow cold

Чай сты́нет. The tea is getting cold.

СТУК-, KNOCK

стук, knock, rap

Разда́лся стук в дверь. There was a knock at the door.

сту́к-нуть, to knock, **rap,** pound, bang

Хозя́ин сту́кнул кулако́м по столу́. The master banged his fist on the table.

стуч-а́ть, to knock, **hammer,** pound

Ти́ше, не стучи́те! Quiet, don't make a noise!

СУД-, JUDGE

суд, court, justice

На него́ по́дали в суд. Proceedings were started against him.

суд-ья́, judge

Судья́ его́ оправда́л. The judge acquitted him.

суд-и́ть, to judge, criticize

Не суди́те так стро́го. Don't criticize so severely.

суд-ь-ба́, destiny, lot

Такова́ моя́ судьба́! Such is my lot.

об-сужд-а́ть, to discuss, consider

Они́ до́лго обсужда́ли э́тот вопро́с. They discussed this matter for a long time.

рас-су́д-ок, reason, mind

Она́ потеря́ла рассу́док. She lost her mind.

T

TA-, SECRET

та-и́ть, to conceal, hide, bear

Вы таи́ли зло́бу про́тив неё. You bore malice against her. (You had a grudge against her.)

та-йко́м, secretly

Он забра́лся сюда́ тайко́м. He came in secretly.

та́-йна, secret, mystery

Я сохраню́ та́йну. I shall keep the secret.

ТВАР-, ТВОР-, CREATE

твар-ь, creature

Бо́жья тварь. God's creature.

твор-е́ц, creator, author	Подража́телей мно́го, а творцо́в ма́ло. There are many imitators, but few creators.
твор-и́ть, to create	Вы твори́те чудеса́. You do wonders. (You work miracles.)
тво́р-чество, creation, genius	Э́то тво́рчество знамени́того писа́теля. This is the work of a well-known writer.
при-тво́р-ный, hypocritical, pretending	На её лице́ притво́рная улы́бка. A hypocritical smile plays on her face.

ТВЕРД-, HARD, FIRM

тверд-е́ть, to become hard, harden	От хо́лода по́чва тверде́ет. The ground hardens from cold.
твёрд-ый, hard	Грани́т твёрдый ка́мень. Granite is a hard stone.
вы́-тверд-ить, to have by heart, master	Он уже́ вы́твердил уро́к. He already has his lesson by heart.
у-тверж-да́ть, to maintain, affirm	Я утвержда́ю что э́то так. I maintain that it is so.

ТЕК-, ТОК-, FLOW, CURRENT

теч-ь (тек-ть), to flow, run, stream, leak	Из кра́на течёт вода́. Water runs from the faucet.
теч-е́ние, course, current	Всё ула́дится с тече́нием вре́мени. In the course of time everything will come out all right.
ис-тек-а́ть, to elapse, expire, bleed	Ра́неный истека́ет кро́вью. The wounded man is bleeding.

ток, current, charge, stream, threshing	Он бы: убит электри́ческим то́ком. He was killed by an electric current.
вос-то́к, east	Мы уезжа́ем на восто́к. We are going east.
ис-то́к, source	Исто́к Во́лги мелково́ден. The source (beginning) of the Volga river is shallow.
ис-то́ч-ник, source, spring, origin, authority	Э́то са́мый ве́рный исто́чник. This is the best source (authority).
по-то́к, stream, torrent	Шуми́т го́рный пото́к. The mountain torrent roars.

ТОК-, LATHE, TURN, SHARP

ток-а́рный, turner's, worked on a lathe	В на́шей дере́вне занима́ются тока́рным ремесло́м. In our village they have taken up the turner's trade.
точ-и́ть, to sharpen, whet, grind	Точи́льщик то́чит ножи́. The grinder sharpens the knives.

ТЕМ-, ТМ-, ТЬМ-, DARK

тем-не́ть, to become dark	Уже́ темне́ет, пора́ домо́й. It is getting dark, it's time to go home.
тем-нота́, darkness	В тако́й темноте́ мо́жно но́гу слома́ть. In this darkness one can break a leg.
тём-ный, dark, shady	У него́ тёмное про́шлое. He has a dark past.
тьм-а, darkness	Там цари́т тьма неве́жества. The darkness of ignorance reigns there.
за-тм-и́ть, to eclipse, shade	Он затми́л всех свои́м умо́м. His wit eclipsed everyone.

за-тм-éние, eclipse

Зáвтра затмéние сóлнца. The eclipse (of the sun) is tomorrow.

в-по-тьм-áх, in the dark

Мы просидéли впотьмáх цéлый час. We stayed in the dark for a whole hour.

по-тём-ки, dark, darkness

Они вы́ехали потёмками. They went off while it was dark.

ТЕП-, ТОП-, WARM

тёп-лый, warm

Вчерá был тёплый день. It was a warm day yesterday.

теп-лúться, to burn, shine

В душé её теплúлся идеалúзм. Idealism was burning in her soul.

теп-лотá, warmth, heat

Держúте это растéние в кóмнатной теплотé. Keep this plant at room temperature.

топ-úть, to heat, put fuel

Он тóпит пéчку. He is heating the stove.

тóп-ливо, fuel

У нас нет тóплива. We have no fuel.

о-топ-лéние, heat, heating

В этом здáнии паровóе отоплéние. In this building there is steam heat.

ТЕР-, ТИР-, ТР-, RUB

тер-éть, to rub, chafe

Воротнúк трёт мне шéю. The collar chafes my neck.

тёр-ка, grater

Отнесúте тёрку на кýхню. Take the grater to the kitchen.

в-тир-а́ться, to insinuate, rub in, ingratiate

Он втира́ется в ва́ше дове́рие. He is ingratiating himself to win yŏur confidence.

с-ти́р-ка, wash, laundry

По понеде́льникам у нас сти́рка. On Mondays we do our laundry.

тр-е́ние, rubbing, friction

Маши́на тепе́рь рабо́тает без тре́ния. The machine works now without friction. (The machine runs smoothly now.)

ТЕРП-, SUFFER

терп-е́ть, to suffer, bear, endure, tolerate

Они́ те́рпят нужду́. They suffer from want.

терп-е́ние, patience

Я потеря́л вся́кое терпе́ние. I have completely lost my patience.

те́рп-кий, tart, sharp, sour

Э́то сли́шком те́рпкое вино́. This wine is too sour.

ТЕС-, (ТѢС)-, ТИС-, CROWD

те́с-ный, tight, close, intimate

Их свя́зывала те́сная дру́жба. Intimate friendship bound them together.

при-тес-ня́ть, to oppress, persecute

Прави́тельство их вся́чески притесня́ет. The government persecutes them in every way.

с-тес-не́ние, constraint, embarrassment

Расскажи́те мне всё без стесне́ния. Tell me everything (and) don't feel embarrassed.

ти́с-кать, to squeeze, cram, to be pushed

Меня́ ти́скали в толпе́. I was pushed in the crowd.

с-ти́с-нуть, to squeeze, clench, set

От бо́ли он сти́снул зу́бы. He clenched his teeth with pain.

ТИХ-, ТЕХ-, (ТѢХ)-, QUIET, AMUSE

тих-ий, calm, quiet

Какáя тихая ночь. What a calm night!

тиш-инá, stillness, quiet, tranquility

Здесь прохлáда и тишинá. It is cool and calm here.

ис-под-тиш-кá, stealthily, in an underhand way, on the sly

У них всё дéлается исподтишкá. They do everything on the sly.

по-тéх-а, fun, amusement

Вот потéха! What fun! (How amusing!)

тéш-ить, to console, rejoice, amuse, please

Он тéшит себя напрáсной надéждой. He consoles himself with an empty hope.

у-тéх-а, pleasure, solace, comfort, joy

Мне не до утéх. I have no time for pleasure.

у-тéш-ить, to console

Дочь утéшила мать. The daughter has consoled her mother.

по-тéш-ный, amusing, ridiculous, funny

У мáльчика потéшный вид. The boy looks funny.

ТК-, ТОЧ-, WEAVE, POINT

тк-ать, to weave

Бáбы ткут полотнó. The peasant women are weaving the linen.

тк-ач, weave

Читáли-ли вы пьéсу "Ткачи"? Have you read the play "The Weavers"?

тк-áцкий, weaving

На ткáцкой фáбрике выдéлывают тóнкую ткань. At the weaving mill fine fabrics are made.

тóч-ка, point, dot, stop, view, aspect

Я не соглáсен с вáшей тóчкой зрéния. I don't agree with your point of view.

тóч-ность, exactness, accuracy

Он сомневáется в тóчности перевóда. He doubts the accuracy of the translation.

тóч-ный, precise, exact

Это егó тóчные словá. These are his exact words.

точ-ь, exactly

Он точь в точь в отцá. He is exactly like his father.

ТЛ-, SPOIL, DECAY, SMOULDER

тл-еть, to decay, smoulder

Жар тлéет под пéплом. The fire smoulders under the ashes.

тл-ен, decay, dust

Всё на землé тлен. Everything on earth is dust.

ТОВАР-, GOODS, COMPANY

товáр, merchandise, goods

Товáр ужé полýчен. The merchandise has already arrived.

товáр-ищ, comrade

Товáрищ Петрóв вошёл в зал. Comrade Petrov entered the hall.

товáр-ный, freight, goods

Товáрный пóезд опоздáл на час. The freight train was an hour late.

ТОЛК-, EXPLAIN, PUSH

толк, meaning, sense, understanding

Он знáет толк в мýзыке. He is a good judge of music.

толк-овáть, to talk, comment, explain

Довóльно толковáть о пустякáх. Stop talking about trifles.

толк-óвый, sensible, bright

Вáня толкóвый мáлый. Vanya is a bright youngster.

толк-а́ть, ⎱ to push, jostle,
толк-ну́ть, ⎰ nudge

Я толкну́л его́ локтём. I nudged him.

толк-отня́, crush, crowd, jostling, bustle

Что там за толкотня́? What is that bustling crowd there?

толк-у́чка, rag-fair

На толку́чке продаю́т ста́рые ве́щи. At the rag-fair they sell secondhand things.

ТОП-, SINK

топ-и́ть, to sink, drown

Ми́на то́пит су́дно. The torpedo is sinking a ship.

тон-у́ть, to drown

Помоги́те, челове́к то́нет! Help! A man is drowning!

по-то́п, flood, deluge

Они́ говори́ли о всеми́рном пото́пе. They were talking about the Flood.

у-то́п-ленник, body of a drowned man

Волна́ вы́бросила уто́пленника на́ берег. A wave brought to the shore the body of a drowned man.

ТОРГ-, TRADE

торг, trade, auction, auction sale

Име́ние про́дали с торго́в. The estate was sold by auction.

торг-ова́ть, to trade, deal, sell

Чем вы торгу́ете? What are you selling? What kind of a trade are you carrying on?

торг-о́вый, trading, business, commercial, mercantile

Торго́вый дом бра́тьев Орло́вых. The mercantile company of the brothers Orlov.

торж-ество́, triumph, victory

Торжество́ доброде́тели над поро́ком. Triumph of virtue over vice.

ТРЕСК-, CRACK

треск, crack, crash	Дéрево упáло с трéском. The tree fell with a crash.
трéс-нуть, to crack, burst	Стеклó трéснуло. The glass cracked.
трещ-áть, to creak, crack, rattle	Мáчта трещи́т от вéтра. The mast creaks in the wind.
трéщ-ина, crack, split	На стенé большáя трéщина. There is a large crack in the wall.

ТРУД-, LABOR

труд, labor, work	Физи́ческий труд полéзен. Physical labor is wholesome.
трýд-ный, difficult	Они́ не поддержáли егó в трýдную минýту. They failed him when he was in a difficult position (in need).
труд-и́ться, to work, labor	Онá всю жизнь труди́лась. She has worked hard all her life.
трýж-еник, worker, hard worker	Он чéстный трýженик наýки. He is an honest and hard-working man of learning (scholar).
у-труждáть, to trouble, in-convenience	Я не хочý вас утруждáть. I do not want to cause you any trouble.

ТУГ-, ТЯГ-, TIGHT, STIFF

туг-óй, tight, stiff	Он туг на расплáту. He is stingy. (He is slow in paying back.)

на-тýг-а, strain, effort	Он заболéл с натýги. He fell ill from too much strain.
туж-и́ть, to grieve, regret	Нéчего вам тужи́ть. You must not grieve. (There is nothing for you to regret.)
тя́г-а, draught, pull, current	В печи́ плоха́я тя́га. There is not enough draught in the stove chimney.
тя-нýть (тяг-нуть), to draw, drag	Рыбаки́ тя́нут сéти. The fishermen are dragging the net.
тяж-ёлый, heavy	Я несý тяжёлый чемода́н. I am carrying a heavy suitcase.
за-тяж-нóй, slow, lingering	Болéзнь приняла́ затяжнóй хара́ктер. The disease is turning into a lingering malady.

ТУСК-, DIM

тýск-лый, dim	Больнóй оки́нул кóмнату тýсклым взгля́дом. The sick man looked round the room with dimmed eyes.
по-туск-нéть, to tarnish, grow dim	Серебрó потускнéло. The silver is tarnished.

У

УЗ-, TIE, BOND, KNOT

ýз-ел, knot	Зачéм вы завяза́ли ýзел? Why did you tie the knot?
ýз-кий, narrow	Здесь óчень ýзкий прохóд. The passage here is very narrow.

у́з-ник, captive, prisoner

Узника повели́ в кре́пость.
They took the prisoner to
the fortress.

об-у́з-а, burden, load

На него́ навали́ли обу́зу.
They heaped a load on him.
(They loaded him with
work.)

УК-, ЫК-, LEARN

на-у́к-а, science

Мы изуча́ем есте́ственные
нау́ки. We are studying
natural sciences.

уч-е́бник, textbook

Куда́ вы положи́ли уче́бник?
Where did you put the
textbook?

уч-е́ние, learning

Уче́ние свет, а неуче́ние
тьма. Learning is light and
ignorance is darkness.

уч-и́тельница, teacher

Вот на́ша учи́тельница.
There is our teacher.

уч-и́ться, to learn, study

Я учу́сь в шко́ле. I go to
school. (I study at school.)

на́в-ык, habit, practice, ex-
perience

У вас нет на́выка к чёрной
рабо́те. You are not used
to manual labor.

не́-уч, ignoramus

Како́й не́уч! What an
ignoramus!

об-ы́ч-ай, custom

Тако́в у них обы́чай. Such
is their custom.

об-ы́ч-ный, customary, usual

Э́то наш обы́чный поря́док.
This is our usual arrangement.

об-ык-нове́нный,   ordinary,
customary, usual

Обыкнове́нно мы обе́даем в
шесть часо́в. Usually we
dine at six.

прив-ы́ч-ка, habit

Привы́чка — втора́я нату́ра.
Habit is (our) second nature.

УМ-, MIND

ум, mind, reason, wit	Ум доро́же де́нег. Mind is dearer than money.
у́м-ный, clever	Она́ у́мная же́нщина. She is a clever woman.
без-у́м-ие, madness	Так поступа́ть — су́щее безу́мие. To act this way is sheer madness.
из-ум-ля́ть,⎫ to surprise, из-ум-и́ть, ⎭ amaze	Ваш посту́пок меня́ изумля́ет. Your conduct surprises me
раз-у́м-ный, sensible	Э́то разу́мный план. This is a sensible plan (project).
ум-е́ть, to be able	Уме́ете-ли вы писа́ть? Can you write?

X

ХВАТ-, ХИТ-, GRASP, SEIZE

хват-а́ть, to grasp	Ма́льчик хвата́ет мяч. The boy grasps the ball.
хват-и́ть, to suffice, be sufficient	У меня́ не хвати́ло де́нег на пое́здку. I did not have sufficient money for the trip.
за-хва́т, seizure, seizing	Рабо́чие ду́мали о захва́те вла́сти. The workmen thought of seizing the power.
с-хва́т-ка, scuffle, skirmish	Ме́жду ни́ми была́ схва́тка. There was a scuffle among them.
по-хит-и́ть, to steal, kidnap	У э́тих люде́й похити́ли ребёнка. The child of these people was kidnapped.

по-хищ-е́ние, theft, abduction, kidnapping

Об э́том похище́нии писа́ли в газе́тах. This kidnapping was written about in the newspapers.

хи́щ-ный, predatory, rapacious

Тигр хи́щное живо́тное. The tiger is a rapacious animal.

вос-хищ-а́ться, to admire, to be delighted

Мы восхища́лись её игро́й. We admired her playing.

ХЛАД-, ХОЛОД-, COLD

о-хлад-и́ть, to cool

Неуда́чи охлади́ли его́ пыл. Failures have cooled his ardor (enthusiasm).

о-хлажд-е́ние, coolness

Ме́жду ни́ми произошло́ охлажде́ние. A coolness sprang up between them.

про-хла́д-ный, cool

В ко́мнате прохла́дно. It is cool in the room.

хо́лод, cold

Стоя́т холода́. We are having cold weather (a cold spell).

холо́д-ный, cold

Да́йте мне холо́дного молока́. Let me have some cold milk.

ХОД-, ШЕД-, GO

ход, course, march, speed, movement, progress

Ему́ не даю́т хо́ду. They hamper his progress. (He does not get on.)

ход-и́ть, to go

Я ча́сто хожу́ в теа́тр. I often go to the theatre.

вос-хо́д, sunrise

Ле́том мы встаём с восхо́дом со́лнца. In summer we get up at sunrise.

вы́-ход-ка, trick, prank, quirk

Каки́е у него́ стра́нные вы́ходки. He has such odd quirks.

при-хо́д, arrival, coming

Мы ждём прихо́да по́езда. We are waiting for the arrival of the train.

проис-ход-и́ть, to take place, happen, go on

Что там происхо́дит? What is going on there?

рас-хо́д, expense, expenditure

У нас больши́е расхо́ды. Our expenses are great.

с-хо́д-ка, meeting

Была́ шу́мная схо́дка. There was a noisy meeting.

у-ход-и́ть, to go away, leave

Я ухожу́, до свида́ния! I am leaving; good-by!

про-шéд-ший, past

Он распла́чивается за всё проше́дшее. He is paying for the past.

на-шéс-твие, invasion

Чита́ли-ли вы о наше́ствии тата́р? Did you read about the Tartar invasion?

путе-шéс-твие, travel, trip, journey

Э́то путеше́ствие меня́ утоми́ло. This trip has tired me.

ХРАН-, ХОРОН-, HIDE, BURY

хран-и́ть, to hide, keep

Она́ уме́ет храни́ть та́йну. She knows how to keep a secret.

пред-о-хран-е́ние, prevention, protection

Вот сре́дство для предохране́ния от просту́ды. Here is a remedy to prevent a cold.

хорон-и́ть, to bury

Вчера́ хорони́ли самоуби́йцу. Yesterday they buried a suicide.

по́-хорон-ы, funeral

Я не пошёл на по́хороны. I did not go to the funeral.

Ц

ЦВЕТ-, (ЦВѢТ)-, COLOR, FLOWER

цвет, color	Какóго цвéта вáше нóвое пальтó? What color is your new coat?
цвет-óк, flower	Онá сорвалá цветóк. She picked a flower.
цвет-очный, flower, flowery, blossom	Дáйте мне фунт цветóчного чáю. Let me have a pound of jasmin tea.
цве-стú, to bloom, flower	Сирéнь цветёт рáнней веснóй. The lilac blooms early in spring.
про-цвет-áть, to thrive	Делá нáши процветáют. Our affairs are thriving. (Our business is thriving.)

ЦЕЛ-, (ЦѢЛ)-, WHOLE

цéл-ый, whole, entire	Онú рабóтают по цéлым дням. They work all day long.
цел-овáть, to kiss	Войскá шли целовáть крест. The troops went to kiss the cross. (The troops went to swear allegiance.)
по-цел-ýй, kiss	Пéрвый поцелýй весны́. The first kiss of springtime.
ис-цел-úть, to cure, heal	Минерáльные воды егó исцелúли. The mineral waters have cured him.

ЦЕН-, (ЦѢН)-, WORTH, VALUE

цен-á, price, value, cost	Вéщи прóданы по высóкой ценé. The things were sold at a high price.

цен-и́ть, to value

Я ценю́ ва́шу дру́жбу. I value your friendship.

драго-це́н-ный, precious

Зо́лото драгоце́нный мета́лл. Gold is a precious metal.

о-це́н-ка, evaluation, estimate

Его́ оце́нка сли́шком низка́. His estimate is too low.

Ч

ЧА-, EXPECT, HOPE

ча́-ять, to expect, hope

Не ча́ял я тако́й встре́чи. I did not expect such a meeting.

не-ча́-янный, unexpected, inadvertent

Он неча́янно разби́л ва́зу. Inadvertently he broke the vase.

от-ча́-яние, despair, despondency

Нельзя́ впада́ть в тако́е отча́яние. You must not let yourself get so desperate.

ЧА-, ЧН-, ЧИН-, START, BEGIN

на-чин-а́ть,

⎱ to begin, start

на-ча́-ть,

Мы начина́ем рабо́тать в во́семь часо́в утра́. We begin our work at eight o'clock in the morning.

Я на́чал писа́ть письмо́. I have started to write a letter.

на-ча́-льник, head, chief

Нача́льник прие́дет в де́вять. The chief will come at nine.

на-чн-ёте, you will begin

Вы ско́ро начнёте говори́ть по-ру́сски. You will soon begin to speak Russian.

ЧАСТ-, PART, LOT

част-ь, part, portion

Они получи́ли то́лько часть насле́дства. They got only a portion of the inheritance.

ча́ст-ный, private

Он про́тив ча́стной со́ственности. He is against private property.

с-ча́ст-ье, luck, happiness

Э́то ва́ше сча́стье! This is your luck! (It is your luck!)

со-у-ча́ст-ие, participation

Он заподо́зрен в соуча́стии в уби́йстве. They suspected his participation in the murder.

у́-част-ь, lot, destiny

Её пости́гла го́рькая у́часть. A sad lot has befallen her.

ЧЕР-, BLACK

чер-не́ть, to look black

Что́-то черне́ло вдали́. There was something black in the distance.

чёр-ный, black

Где мой чёрный каранда́ш? Where is my black pencil?

чер-н-и́ла, ink

Вот кра́сные черни́ла. Here is the red ink.

чер-н-и́ть, to blackmail, slander

Не черни́те меня́ напра́сно. Don't slander me for no cause.

чер-но-ви́к, draft

Черновик отослан реда́ктору. The draft is sent to the editor.

ЧЕР(К)-, SCRIBBLE

чёр-к-ать,
чер-к-ну́ть, } to scribble, jot down, write

Что вы там чёркаете? What are you scribbling there?

Черкни́те мне не́сколько слов. Write (scribble) me a few words.

за-чёр-к-ивать, to cross, cross out

Учи́тель зачёркивает оши́бки. The teacher crosses out the mistakes.

о́-чер-к, essay

Ваш о́черк мне понра́вился. I liked your essay.

по́-чер-к, handwriting

У неё неразбо́рчивый по́черк. She has a poor handwriting.

ЧЕР(Т)-, DRAW

черт-а́, line, trait

Они́ жи́ли на пограни́чной черте́. They lived at the frontier. (They lived on the border line.)

черт-ёж, plan, sketch, draft, table

В кни́ге мно́го чертежéй. There are many drafts (tables) in the book.

черт-и́ть, to draw, trace, sketch

Инжене́р че́ртит план. The engineer is drawing a map.

чер-ч-е́ние, drawing, draft

Он занима́ется черче́нием. He is making a draft.

ЧИН-, RANK, CAUSE

чин, rank

Ему́ да́ли но́вый чин. They promoted him to a new rank.

чин-о́в-ник, official, clerk

В кабине́т вошёл чино́вник. An official walked into the office.

чин-и́ть, to cause

Никому́ я зла не чини́л. I have not done harm to anyone.

за-чи́н-щик, instigator

Он был среди́ зачи́нщиков. He was among the instigators.

под-чин-е́ние, subjection, subordination

Генера́л держа́л во́йско в подчине́нии. The general kept the troops in subordination.

при-чи́на, cause

Всему́ своя́ причи́на. Everything has its own cause.

со-чин-е́ние, composition, essay

За́втра мне на́до пода́ть сочине́ние. Tomorrow I must hand in the essay.

ЧИСТ-, CLEAN

чи́ст-ый, clean

На столе́ чи́стая ска́терть. There is a clean cloth on the table.

чи́ст-ить, to clean, polish

Сапо́жник чи́стит боти́нки. The shoemaker is polishing the shoes.

чист-ота́, cleanliness, neatness

Кака́я у них чистота́! How neat they are! (How clean it is in their house!)

рас-чищ-а́ть, to clear away

Садо́вник расчища́ет доро́жку са́да. The gardener clears the path in the garden.

ЧТ-, ЧИТ-, ЧЕТ-, READ, COUNT

чт-е́ние, reading

Я провожу́ вечера́ за чте́нием. I spend my evenings reading.

по-чт-е́ние, respect, esteem, honor

Мое почте́ние! My compliments! (My respects!)

чт-ить, to respect, esteem	Дети чтут своих родителей. The children respect their parents.
чит-áть, to read	Читáйте дáльше пожáлуй-ста! Read farther, please!
вы-чит-áние, deduction, sub-traction	Мой брат прохóдит вычитá-ние. My brother is learn-ing subtraction.
чет-á, match, equal	Он вам не четá. He is no match for you.
по-чёт, honor, respect	Писáтеля проводúли с почё-том. The writer was honored with a farewell party.
с-чёт, account, bill	Принесúте счёт. Bring the bill.

ЧУ-, FEEL

чý-в-ство, feeling, sense, sensa-tion	Им овладéло чýвство жáло-сти. Pity overcame him.
по-чý-в-ствовать, to feel	Я почýвствовал себя дýрно. I felt dizzy.
чý-т-кий, sensitive	Онá чýткий человéк. She is sensitive.
пред-чý-в-ствие, premonition	Предчýвствие меня не обма-нýло. The premonition did not deceive me.
со-чý-в-ствие, sympathy, compassion	Он вы́слушал её с сочýв-ствием. He listened to her with sympathy. (He heard her out with sympathy.)

ЧУД-, ЧУЖ-, WONDER, STRANGE

чýд-о, wonder	Мнóго чудéс на свéте. There are many wonders in the world.

чуд-а́к, queer fellow

Како́й вы чуда́к! What a queer person (fellow) you are!

чуд-е́сный, wonderful

Вчера́ была́ чуде́сная пого́да. Yesterday the weather was wonderful.

чуд-о́вище, monster

Мно́го говори́ли о морско́м чудо́вище.   There were many talks about the sea monster.

чуж-о́й, strange, stranger

Како́й-то чужо́й челове́к пришёл. A stranger came.

чуж-д-а́ться, to shun

Он всех чужда́ется.   He shuns everybody.

чуж-би́на, foreign country

Нам пришло́сь жить на чужби́не. We had to live in a foreign country.

чуж-е-зе́мец, alien, foreigner

Он счита́ет себя́ чужезе́мцем. He regards himself as an alien.

Ш

ШЕД-, SEE: ХОД-

ШИБ-, HIT, MISS

о-ши́б-ка, mistake, error

Вы сде́лали мно́го оши́бок. You have made many errors.

о-шиб-а́ться,
⎱ to err, to be
⎰ mistaken
о-шиб-и́ться,

Не ошиба́етесь-ли вы? Are you not mistaken?

Да, я оши́бся. Yes, I am mistaken. (I am wrong.)

о-ши́б-очный, erroneous, mistaken

Э́то оши́бочное мне́ние.   It is a mistaken opinion.

у-шиб-и́ть, to hit, hurt

Я уши́бла но́гу. I have hurt my foot.

Щ

ЩАД-, ЩЕД-, MERCY, SPARE. GENEROUS

щад-и́ть, to spare, have mercy

Она́ щади́т его́ самолю́бие. She spares his ambition.

по-щад-а, mercy, pardon

Ему́ нет поща́ды. There is no pardon for him.

бес-по-ща́д-ный, unmerciful, cruel

Всех беспоща́дно поби́ли. They were all cruelly beaten.

ще́д-рый, generous

Он раздава́л де́ньги ще́дрой руко́й. He gave the money away with a generous hand.

ще́д-рость, generosity

Его́ ще́дрость меня́ глубоко́. тро́нула. His generosity deeply touched me.

ЩИТ-, PROTECT, SHIELD

щит, shield

На стене́ виси́т стари́нный щит. An ancient shield hangs on the wall.

за-щи́т-а, protection

Я обраща́юсь к ва́шей защи́те. I apply to you for protection.

за-щи́т-ник, lawyer, counsel for the defense

Защи́тник вы́ступил с ре́чью. The lawyer came out with a speech.

за-щищ-а́ть to defend

Почему́ вы всегда́ его́ защища́ете. Why do you defend him always?

Я

Я-, SEE: ЕМ-, ИМ-

ЯВ-, APPEAR

яв-ля́ться, }to appear, come
яв-и́ться, }

У меня́ яви́лась мысль по-
е́хать заграни́цу. I thought
of going abroad.

яв-ле́ние, appearance, phenomenon

Коме́та — ре́дкое явле́ние
приро́ды. The comet is a
rare phenomenon.

я́в-ный, obvious, evident

Э́то я́вная ложь. This is an
obvious lie.

за-яв-ле́ние, statement, depo-
sition, declaration

Вам на́до пода́ть заявле́ние.
You must file a statement.

об'-яв-ле́ние, advertisement

Помести́те об'явле́ние в га-
зе́те. Place an advertisement in the newspaper.

ЯС-, CLEAR

яс-не́ть, to become clear,
clear up

Гроза́ прохо́дит, уже́ ясне́ет.
The storm is passing, it is
already clearing.

я́с-ный, clear, bright

Настаёт я́сный день. The
bright (clear) day is be-
ginning.

вы́-яс-нить, to ascertain, find
out

Нам необходи́мо вы́яснить в
чём тут затрудне́ние. We
must find out what is the
difficulty.

об'-яс-не́ние, explanation

Она́ мо́лча вы́слушала моё
об'ясне́ние. She silently
listened to my explanation.

про-яс-ня́ться, to clear up

Пого́да проясня́ется. The
weather is clearing up.

EXERCISES FOR PRACTICE

1

Form two derivatives with each of the following roots and use them in original sentences—

Вид; дом; лес; лист; мир; род; сад; труд; ум; хо́лод.

2

Resolve into their elements the following words, naming each root and the prefixes and suffixes in combination with it—

Вопро́с; высота́; выступа́ть; глубина́; держа́ть; замести́тель; кра́сный; ме́стность; отнести́; признаёт; благоро́дство; рожде́ние; ра́доваться; обще́ственный; собира́ть; вы́борный; собо́р; по́дданство; ре́зкость; избра́ние; разбира́тельство.

3

Underline the prefixes and suffixes in the following words—

Ка́менщик рабо́тал с утра́ до ве́чера. Перево́дчик перевёл ве́рно, а перепи́счик наде́лал мно́го оши́бок. Набо́рщик око́нчил свою́ рабо́ту. Лётчики спасли́ матро́сов. На стро́йке рабо́тают пло́тники, печники́ и стеко́льщики. Кто принёс газе́ту? Мой прия́тель занёс кни́гу. Отнеси́те э́то домо́й. Тут вход, а там вы́ход. Посмотри́те на захо́д со́лнца. Перехо́д че́рез го́ры был тру́ден. Не подходи́те к нему́. Подпиши́тесь, пожа́луйста. Закрича́ть; занести́; записа́ть.

4

Form new words with the prefixes in parentheses—

игра́ть (раз-); изве́стный (без-); иска́ть (от-); иду́ (пред-); интере́сный (без-). На́до иска́ть (под-) но́вые приме́ры. В э́той рабо́те мо́жно отме́тить ряд интере́сных (не-, без-) улучше́ний. Ва́ши замеча́ния игра́ют (с-) ва́жную роль в на́шем де́ле.

5

Underline the roots in the following words and use each of them in a sentence—

Гора́; го́рка; го́рец; го́рный; приго́рок. Горе́ть; загоре́ться; вы́гореть; ога́рок; прига́р; горя́чий; го́рький; горчи́ца; го́ре; грусть; выпи́сывать; преподава́тельница; стекля́нный; ру́сский; учи́тельский; дать; изда́ние; прида́ное; пода́тель; 'разда́ча; распрода́жа.

6

Add the prefixes—

(1) раз-, разо-, рас- to the words:
брать; верну́ть; вести́; дать; положи́ть; рабо́тать; сказа́ть; смотре́ть; счита́ть; цвет.

(2) без-, бес- to the words:
вре́дный; земе́льный; коне́чный; мяте́жный: о́бразный; парти́йный; спо́рный; чи́сленный.

(3) из-, изо-, ис- to the words:
бежа́ть; бить; влечь; гнуть; жа́рить; лома́ть; пра́вить; пыта́ть; рвать; тра́тить.

(4) воз-, вос-, вз-, взо-, вс- to the words:
волнова́ться; де́лать; кли́кнуть; мути́ть; ненави́деть; пита́ть; по́мнить; приня́ть; станови́ть; ходи́ть.

7

Add the prefix при-, пре-, or пере- to the following words—
бить; быва́ть; вози́ть; восходи́ть; говори́ть; де́лать; ду́мать; знать; зре́ние; иму́щество; нести́; образова́ние; обрета́ть; останови́ть; подня́ть; сле́довать; стра́стный; учи́ть.

8

Form compounds from the following words—
земля́, ме́рить; кра́сная, а́рмия; жизнь, ра́дость; да́льний, восто́к; про́тив, поста́вить; сам, кри́тика; овца́, води́ть; пу́ля, мета́ть; путь, ше́ствие; вода́, ла́зить; вода́, проводи́ть; о́чи, ви́деть; пять, лет; три, эта́ж; во́семь, лет; три, ме́сяц; де́сять, рубле́й; свой, вре́мя; сам, вари́ть; труд, люби́ть.

Examples: земля́, ме́рить: землеме́р; кра́сная а́рмия: красноарме́ец.

9

Explain the compounds in the following three passages—

Земля́ на Укра́ине плодоро́дна, покры́та то́лстым сло́ем чернозёма. Здесь земледе́лие — гла́вное заня́тие жи́телей. Населе́ние Укра́ины занима́ется та́кже пчелово́-дством, скотово́дством, осо́бенно овцево́дством. Укра́ина соединена́ железнодоро́жными ли́ниями с черномо́рскими порта́ми.

10

Крот весьма́ трудолюби́вый землеко́п. Свои́ми листооб-ра́зными ла́пами он ро́ет в земле́ о́чень дли́нные хо́ды. Крот живо́тное червоя́дное и насекомоя́дное. Э́тим он прино́сит земле́де́льцу и садо́внику по́льзу.

11

Парохо́д идёт с по́мощью па́ра. Парово́з во́зит с по́мощью па́ра. Хлеборо́дный год—э́то год, когда́ хоро́ший урожа́й. Дровосе́ку ну́жен топо́р. Рыболо́в ло́вит ры́бу. Земле-трясе́ние разру́шило не́сколько домо́в. Вчера́ произошло́ кораблекруше́ние. У мои́х ро́дственников лесопи́льный заво́д. Говоря́т, что во мно́гих колхо́зах хорошо́ поста́влено животново́дство, курово́дство, овцево́дство и свиново́дство.

12

Underline the suffixes and the endings in the words of this exercise and the following—

Краснова́тый; чернова́тый; ма́ленький; пи́сьменный; у́стный; ки́слый; речи́стый; у́мный; учи́тельский. Здо-ро́вье велича́йшее бла́го. Волк злейший враг челове́ка. Морска́я вода́ име́ет иногда́ синева́тый, а иногда́ зелено-ва́тый цвет. Мы шли по песча́ному бе́регу реки́. Соба́ка верне́йший друг челове́ка.

13

Э́то был оди́н из великоле́пнейших садо́в в све́те. Он занима́л огро́мнейшее простра́нство, и сам садо́вник не знал ему́ конца́. В саду́ росли́ разнообра́знейшие дере́вья. По дере́вьям порха́ли краси́вейшие пти́цы и пе́ли восхи-ти́тельнейшие пе́сни. Но драгоце́ннейшим украше́нием всего́ са́да был солове́й. Он пел так превосхо́дно, что иностра́нцы наро́чно приезжа́ли его́ слу́шать.

14

Give the diminutives of

Дом; голова́; цепь; ме́сто; ча́шка; крыло́; со́лнце;
Ве́ра; Лёва; изба́; ко́локол; цвето́к; Со́ня; кни́га;
цвет; молото́к; луг; лес; плато́к; го́лос; кусо́к.

Use them in sentences.

15

Form as many derivatives as you can—

Бе́рег; встре́тить; друг; нау́ка; кула́к; во́здух; страх;
свет; иска́ть; суди́ть; крича́ть; род.

Use them in sentences.

16

Underline the roots and the prefixes—

Нёс, нёс, да не донёс. Внести́-то внесёт, а как вы́нести?
Кто э́то принёс? Мой прия́тель занёс кни́гу. Отнеси́те
э́тот паке́т домо́й. Она́ принесла́ слова́рь из библиоте́ки.
Ма́льчик поднёс ло́жку ко рту.
Тут вход, а там вы́ход. Наблюда́й восхо́д и захо́д со́лнца.
Перехо́д че́рез го́ру был тру́ден. Не подходи́те к ней.
Он прихо́дит к ним ка́ждый ве́чер. Сожале́ю, что она́
уже́ ушла́.

17

Underline the prefixes—

Нет пра́вила без исключе́ния. Вся́кий избира́ет дру́га по
своему́ нра́ву. Он всё рассказа́л, но не разма́зал. Ма́слом
ка́ши не испо́ртишь. От бессо́нницы трудо́м ле́чатся.
Бесконе́чная печа́ль его́ меня́ беспоко́ит. Бездо́нную
бо́чку не напо́лнишь. У си́льного всегда́ бесси́льный
винова́т. Беззу́бому тру́дно разжева́ть сухо́й хлеб. Я
истра́тил всё де́ньги. Он си́льно иззя́б. Мы дади́м беспла́т-
ный спекта́кль. Расписа́ние уро́ков разрабо́тано учи́телем.

18

Underline the prefixes and suffixes—

Нали́чность. Дове́рие. На́бережная. Открове́нность.
Новорождённый. Расчища́ть. Засвиде́тельствованный.
Раста́лкивать. Извеща́емый. Представля́ть. Расто́ржен-
ный. Предводи́тельница. Накра́шенный. Неизбе́жность.
Приходя́щий. Чита́ющий.

19

Explain the following compounds—

Руководи́тель, морепла́ватель, путеводи́тель, рудоко́п, рыбо-
ло́в, землеме́р, мышело́вка, сердцебие́ние, жизнеописа́ние,
небоскрёб, ледохо́д, светлозелёный, белоку́рый, черного-
ло́вый, многолю́дный, подобостра́стный, прошлого́дний,
птицело́в.

Underline the roots in the following passage—

Чу́ден Днепр при ти́хой пого́де, когда́ во́льно и пла́вно
мчит сквозь леса́ и го́ры по́лные во́ды свои́. Ни зашелохнёт,
ни прогреми́т: гляди́шь и не зна́ешь, идёт и́ли не идёт
его́ велича́вая ширина́, и чу́дится, бу́дто весь вы́лит он из
стекла́, и бу́дто голуба́я зерка́льная доро́га, без ме́ры в
ширину́, без конца́ в длину́, ре́ет и вьётся по зелёному
ми́ру. Лю́бо тогда́ и жа́ркому со́лнцу огляде́ться с вышины́
и погрузи́ть лучи́ в хо́лод стекля́нных вод, и прибре́жным
леса́м я́рко отрази́ться в во́дах. Зеленоку́дрые! они́
толпя́тся вме́сте с полевы́ми цвета́ми к во́дам и, накло-
ни́вшись, глядя́т в них и не наглядя́тся, и не налюбу́ются
све́тлым свои́м зра́ком, и усмеха́ются ему́, и приве́тствуют
его́, кива́я ветвя́ми; в середи́ну же Днепра́ они́ не сме́ют
гля́нуть: никто́, кро́ме со́лнца и голубо́го не́ба, не гляди́т
в него́; ре́дкая пти́ца долети́т до середи́ны Днепра́. Пы́ш-
ный! ему́ нет ра́вной реки́ в ми́ре.
(Го́голь.)

INDEX OF WORDS

Г

INDEX OF ROOTS

LANGUAGE AND REFERENCE BOOKS

Dictionaries and References
VOX Spanish and English Dictionaries
Cervantes-Walls Spanish and English Dictionary
Klett German and English Dictionary
NTC's New College French & English Dictionary
NTC's New College Greek & English Dictionary
Zanichelli New College Italian & English Dictionary
Zanichelli Super-Mini Italian & English Dictionary
NTC's Dictionary of Spanish False Cognates
NTC's Dictionary of German False Cognates
NTC's Dictionary of *Faux Amis*
NTC's American Idioms Dictionary
NTC's Dictionary of American Slang and
  Colloquial Expressions
Forbidden American English
Essential American Idioms
Contemporary American Slang
Everyday American English Dictionary
Everyday American Phrases in Content
Beginner's Dictionary of American English Usage
NTC's Dictionary of Grammar Terminology
Robin Hyman's Dictionary of Quotations
Guide to Better English Spelling
303 Dumb Spelling Mistakes
NTC's Dictionary of Literary Terms
The Writer's Handbook
Diccionario Inglés
El Diccionario Básico Norteamericano
British/American Language Dictionary
The French-Speaking World
The Spanish-Speaking World
Guide to Spanish Idioms
Guide to German Idioms
Guide to French Idioms
101 Japanese Idioms
Au courant
Guide to Correspondence in Spanish
Guide to Correspondence in French
Español para los Hispanos
Business Russian
Yes! You Can Learn a Foreign Language
Japanese in Plain English
Korean in Plain English
Easy Chinese Phrasebook and Dictionary
Japan Today!
Everything Japanese
Easy Hiragana
Easy Katakana
Easy Kana Workbook
The Wiedza Powszechna Compact Polish & English
  Dictionary

Picture Dictionaries
English; French; Spanish; German

Let's Learn...Picture Dictionaries
English, Spanish, French, German, Italian

Verb References
Complete Handbook of Spanish Verbs
Complete Handbook of Russian Verbs
Spanish Verb Drills
French Verb Drills
German Verb Drills

Grammar References
Spanish Verbs and Essentials of Grammar
Nice 'n Easy Spanish Grammar
French Verbs and Essentials of Grammar
Real French
Nice 'n Easy French Grammar
German Verbs and Essentials of Grammar
Nice 'n Easy German Grammar
Italian Verbs and Essentials of Grammar
Essentials of Russian Grammar
Essentials of English Grammar
Roots of the Russian Language
Reading and Translating Contemporary Russian
Essentials of Latin Grammar
Swedish Verbs and Essentials of Grammar

Welcome to...Books
Spain, France, Ancient Greece, Ancient Rome

Language Programs: Audio and Video
Just Listen 'n Learn: Spanish, French, Italian, German,
  Greek
Just Listen 'n Learn PLUS: Spanish, French, German
Speak French
Speak Spanish
Speak German
Practice & Improve Your...Spanish, French, Italian,
  German
Practice & Improve Your...Spanish PLUS, French PLUS,
  Italian PLUS, German PLUS
Improve Your...Spanish, French, Italian, German: The
  P & I Method
Conversational...in 7 Days: Spanish, French, German,
  Italian, Portuguese, Greek, Russian, Japanese, Thai
Everyday Japanese
Japanese for Children
Nissan's Business Japanese
Contemporary Business Japanese
Basic French Conversation
Basic Spanish Conversation
Everyday Hebrew
VideoPassport in French and Spanish
How to Pronounce Russian Correctly
How to Pronounce Spanish Correctly
How to Pronounce French Correctly
How to Pronounce Italian Correctly
How to Pronounce Japanese Correctly
L'Express: Ainsi va la France
L'Express: Aujourd'hui la France
Der Spiegel: Aktuelle Themen in der Bundesrepublik
  Deutschland
Listen and Say It Right in English
Once Upon a Time in Spanish, French, German
Let's Sing & Learn in French & Spanish

"Just Enough" Phrase Books
Chinese, Dutch, French, German, Greek, Hebrew,
  Hungarian, Italian, Japanese, Portuguese, Russian,
  Scandinavian, Serbo-Croat, Spanish
Business French, Business German, Business Spanish

Language Game and Humor Books
Easy French Vocabulary Games
Easy French Crossword Puzzles
Easy French Word Games and Puzzles
Easy French Grammar Puzzles
Easy Spanish Word Power Games
Easy Spanish Crossword Puzzles
Easy Spanish Vocabulary Puzzles
Easy French Word Games and Puzzles
Easy French Culture Games
Easy German Crossword Puzzles
Easy Italian Crossword Puzzles
Let's Learn about Series: Italy, France, Germany, Spain,
  America
Let's Learn Coloring Books in Spanish, French, German,
  Italian, English
Let's Learn...Spanish, French, German, Italian, English
  Coloring Book-Audiocassette Package
My World in...Coloring Books: Spanish, French,
  German, Italian
German à la Cartoon
Spanish à la Cartoon
French à la Cartoon
101 American English Idioms
El alfabeto
L'alphabet

Getting Started Books
Introductory language books in Spanish, French,
  German, Italian

Ticket to...Series
France, Germany, Spain, Italy (Guide and audiocassette)

Getting to Know...Series
France, Germany, Spain, Italy,
  Mexico, United States

PASSPORT BOOKS
a division of *NTC Publishing Group*
Lincolnwood, Illinois USA